DD 120 .S65 C
Carr, Edward Hallett
German-Soviet relations
between the two World Wars

GERMAN–SOVIET RELATIONS
BETWEEN THE TWO WORLD WARS
1919–1939

LONDON: GEOFFREY CUMBERLEGE
OXFORD UNIVERSITY PRESS

GERMAN–SOVIET RELATIONS BETWEEN THE TWO WORLD WARS, 1919–1939

BY

EDWARD HALLETT CARR

GREENWOOD PRESS, PUBLISHERS
WESTPORT, CONNECTICUT

Library of Congress Cataloging in Publication Data

Carr, Edward Hallett, 1892-
    German-Soviet relations between the two World Wars,
1919-1939.

        Reprint. Originally published: Baltimore : Johns
Hopkins Press, 1951. (The Albert Shaw lectures on
diplomatic history ; 1951)
        Bibliography: p.
        Includes index.
        1. Germany--Foreign relations--Soviet Union.
2. Soviet Union--Foreign relations--Germany.
3. Soviet Union--Foreign relations--1917-1945.
4. Germany--Foreign relations--1918-1933. 5. Germany
--Foreign relations--1933-1945. I. Title.
II. Series: Albert Shaw lectures on diplomatic history ;
1951.
DD120.S65C37 1983   327.43047   83-12572
ISBN 0-313-24117-1 (lib. bdg.)

Copyright 1951, The Johns Hopkins Press

Reprinted with the permission of The Johns Hopkins University Press

Reprinted in 1983 by Greenwood Press
A division of Congressional Information Service, Inc.
88 Post Road West, Westport, Connecticut 06881

Printed in the United States of America

10 9 8 7 6 5 4 3 2 1

PREFACE

The six Albert Shaw Lectures on Diplomatic History delivered in The Johns Hopkins University in February and March 1951 form the six chapters of this volume. A few short passages omitted in delivery for lack of time have been restored to their place; otherwise the lectures are printed here substantially in their spoken form. I should like to take this opportunity to express my warm appreciation of the honor conferred on me by the invitation to add a British name to the long list of distinguished lecturers who have participated in this series, and of the friendly and widespread hospitality extended to me during my visit to Baltimore.

Certain special debts incurred in the preparation of these lectures must also be acknowledged. Mr. Gustav Hilger, who was in Moscow throughout almost the whole period covered by this volume as member of the official German mission and later of the German Embassy, put at my disposal his abundant recollections and impressions of German-Soviet diplomatic relations; Mr. G. W. F. Hallgarten, whose article in the *Journal of Modern History* cited in the Note on Sources at the end of the volume was the first independent study of German-Soviet military relations based on the unpublished Seeckt papers, generously allowed me to read his notes and manuscripts and helped me to clear up many doubtful points; and I have also been enabled to profit from the untiring research of Mr. Lionel Kochan, who was recently awarded the degree of Ph. D. by the University of London for an able, though as yet unpublished, thesis on " German-Russian Relations 1921-1934." While none of these must be held responsible for any errors of fact or opinion committed in this volume, they have all given me assistance for which I am deeply grateful.

Whatever light may be shed by this study on current problems, it was not originally inspired by any topical interest. It is part of the preparatory work undertaken for the third volume of my history *The Bolshevik Revolution 1917-1923*, which should be ready for publication next year. Some of the material used in the latter part of Chapter VI had already appeared in two articles by the author " From Munich to Moscow " in *Soviet Studies*, Vol. 1, Nos. 1 and 2 (June and October 1949).

E. H. Carr

20 May, 1951

CONTENTS

		PAGE
I.	THE SETTING AND THE ISSUES	1
II.	RUSSIA, GERMANY AND WORLD REVOLUTION	25
III.	THE ROAD TO RAPALLO	48
IV.	GERMANY FACES BOTH WAYS	67
V.	THE END OF WEIMAR	91
VI.	HITLER AND STALIN	114
	NOTE ON SOURCES	138
	INDEX	143

GERMAN–SOVIET RELATIONS
BETWEEN THE TWO WORLD WARS
1919–1939

CHAPTER I

THE SETTING AND THE ISSUES

FREDERICK THE GREAT of Prussia, forewarned by
his experience of fighting the Russians in the Seven
Years' War, advised his successors to "cultivate the
friendship of these barbarians." The advice was successfully and fruitfully followed for a century and a half. The
Russian victory over Napoleon was the prelude to the
liberation of Prussia. The benevolent neutrality of Russia
was a condition of the Prussian victory over Austria in
1866 and over France in 1871. Russian friendship was a
cornerstone of Bismarck's system; and Bismarck records
how Kaiser William I on his death-bed, mistaking the Iron
Chancellor for his grandson and future successor, William
II, murmured: "Always keep in touch with the Russian
emperor; there no conflict is necessary." These precepts
were neglected by William II in 1914 and by Adolf Hitler
in 1941 — on both occasions with disastrous consequences
for Germany. Throughout this time German friendship
had seemed an equally important asset to Russia. The
Romanov dynasty had German blood in its veins and
intermarried assiduously with German royal and princely
houses; men of German origin enjoyed rapid preferment
at court and in the imperial service. It was not through
the will of Russia that war with Germany occurred in

1

1914 or, still less, in 1941. During the past two centuries German-Russian relations have been a key-point in the international politics of the European continent. The chapters that follow are concerned with these relations over the two decades from the downfall of the Hohenzollerns, just a year after the Bolshevik revolution, at the end of the first world war to the outbreak of the second world war in 1939.

When William II fled to Holland on November 9, 1918, and the German republican government two days later signed the armistice with the Allies, there was no German representative in Moscow and no Soviet representative in Berlin. Mirbach, the German Ambassador sent to Moscow after Brest-Litovsk, had been murdered by the Left Social-Revolutionaries — not by the Bolsheviks — at the beginning of July 1918. His successor Helfferich stayed only three weeks and left, fearing to share Mirbach's fate; and this time the German Government, already facing defeat in the west, did not think it worth its while to replace him. Meanwhile Joffe, the Soviet Ambassador in Berlin, read the signs of Germany's approaching collapse and redoubled his revolutionary propaganda and his subsidies to the German Left. On the very eve of the final collapse, the German imperial government indulged in a last gesture of righteous indignation which may, as the Russians suspected, have been a last desperate attempt to placate its western conquerors. No trouble was taken to collect genuine evidence of the Soviet Ambassador's subversive activities. The police planted some forged revolutionary broadsheets in diplomatic baggage consigned to him, and saw to it that a trunk accidentally burst open in transport.

On the strength of this faked evidence, but on the perfectly correct charge of conducting propaganda against the government to which he was accredited, Joffe was given his passports and depatched with his staff in a special train to the frontier. The date was November 6, 1918. When the Kaiser abdicated three days later, Joffe was at the German-Russian frontier. He waited there for some days in the confident expectation that the German revolutionary government would recall him to Berlin.

In Moscow nobody doubted that the downfall of the monarchy under the impact of defeat was the beginning of the revolution in Germany and, thereafter, in the rest of Europe — the long awaited second and crowning instalment of the proletarian revolution begun in Russia in November 1917. On November 1, 1918, *Pravda* greeted the symptoms of imminent collapse with the banner headline " The World Revolution Has Begun." Workers and Soldiers' Councils sprang up in direct imitation of the Russian Soviets in the principal German centers. When the Kaiser fell, a congress of Berlin Soviets voted into power a provisional government consisting of six People's Commissars; and an All-German Congress of Workers' and Soldiers' Councils was convened to meet in Berlin. These signs were read in Moscow as proof of what already seemed self-evident to disciples of Marx — that the German and Russian revolutions were about to join hands and together sweep triumphantly westwards. The All-Russian Central Executive Committee — the standing organ of the All-Russian Congress of Soviets — formally annulled the Brest-Litovsk Treaty, and nominated Bukharin, Joffe, Rakovsky, Ignatov and Radek as delegates to convey its greetings to the first All-German Congress. In addition to a copious flow of greetings and exhortations by press and radio an immediate offer was made by long-distance telephone to the German People's Commissars of two trainloads of grain to meet the food shortage in the German cities.

The reception of this offer was an effective damper to Soviet enthusiasm. After a week of embarrassed silence, the reply came expressing thanks for the gesture, but explaining that the United States had promised to deliver enough grain to Germany to maintain existing rations till the next harvest. The German revolutionary government had been confronted in the first days of its existence with a practical choice between east and west. The paltry two trainloads from Moscow were weighed against the prospects of trans-Atlantic abundance; it would have been quixotic to accept the Soviet pittance at the risk of antagonising Washington and the western allies. The reply was felt at Moscow as a slap in the face and as a proof that the so-called socialist rulers of Germany preferred the fleshpots of capitalism to the international solidarity of the proletarian revolution. The insult was made worse when the German Government refused to reinstate Joffe as ambassador, and turned back at the frontier the Russian delegation to the All-German Congress. Radek, by origin a Jew from Austrian Poland, who was perfectly at home in Russian, Polish and German and incorrectly fluent in three or four other languages, disguised himself as an Austrian prisoner of war and got through illicitly to Berlin. The other delegates returned disconsolately to Moscow.

The pained surprise which these events evoked showed

how little understanding there was in Moscow of what was happening in Berlin. The German political situation resulting from the collapse of November 1918 was exceedingly complex; and its complexity was reflected in a bewildering variety of attitudes towards Soviet Russia. These attitudes defined themselves gradually, and throughout 1919 were subject to every kind of doubt and fluctuation. But Germany's position between east and west and the enforced choice between them on current issues of policy made it impossible to leave the question in abeyance. The main lines along which different parties and groups divided quickly began to emerge.

The German Social-Democratic Party, the largest organized party in the country, was also the most strongly anti-Russian force in German politics. Hostility to Russia had been the most popular motive invoked to justify the volte-face of the Social-Democrats in August 1914 when, in defiance of all previous party declarations and programmes, they had come out in support of the national war effort; and this deep-seated and traditional hostility did not vanish overnight with the change of regime in Russia. For German workers, and for most of their leaders, the Russians were still a backward and barbarous people, without efficiency, without education and without a serious workers' or trade union movement. The rallying of the German Social-Democratic Party to the cause of national solidarity in the war had accentuated and completed its evolution, already in progress before the war, from a revolutionary to a reformist party — a party that sought to capture and use the state, not to overthrow it. Alone among German political parties the Social-Demo-

cratic Party seemed in 1919 to have the makings of a
radical or liberal party in the western sense; and it was to
the Social-Democrats, once more almost alone in Germany,
that the Wilsonian programme of liberal democracy,
national self-determination and a League of Nations as
the custodian of peace made any serious appeal. The
Social-Democratic Party was from the first, and remained
throughout the period of the Weimar republic, consistently
western rather than eastern in outlook.

The Independent Social-Democratic Party had split off
from the Social-Democrats in 1917 on the issue of support
for the war. It comprized within its ranks a small group,
composed mainly of intellectuals, which called itself the
Spartakusbund and professed an actively revolutionary
Marxist programme. Apart from the Spartakusbund, which
made itself famous for its trenchant clandestine revolutionary propaganda, the Ind' pendent Social-Democrats
were more pacifist than revolutionary in attitude. The
mood of many German workers had been set towards
revolution while revolution seemed the way to peace. But,
once the war was over, they cared more for order than
revolution, and turned a ready ear to Wilsonian propaganda of peace through democracy. The Independent
Social-Democratic Party had derived its strength from
opposition to the war; and there was now little but the
past to divide its Right and non-revolutionary wing from
the Social-Democrats. The German Council of People's
Commissars was composed of six members, three Social-
Democrats and three Independent Social-Democrats. It
was the Independent Social-Democrat Haase, who, being
in charge of foreign affairs, actually communicated to

Moscow the refusal to accept the proffered grain; and the Independent Social-Democrat leaders, Kautsky, Hilferding and Haase were among the bitterest and most persistent German critics of the Bolshevik regime. The Social-Democratic Party and the Right Wing of the Independent Social-Democratic Party, together with the Left Wing of the Catholic Centre, were the only organized parties under the Weimar republic professing an ideology which was neither Bolshevik nor German nationalist and owed something to western inspiration and western models. Unfortunately these ideas were too lightly rooted in the German tradition to withstand the storms ahead.

While the Right Wing of the Independent Social-Democrats gravitated slowly back towards its original home in the Social-Democratic Party, the Spartakusbund transformed itself into the German Communist Party, which held its founding congress on the last day of 1918. Its two outstanding leaders were Rosa Luxemburg, the main intellectual driving force of the Spartakusbund, and Karl Liebknecht, a courageous leader rather than a profound thinker, whose widespread popularity among the workers had been earned by his solitary vote against war credits in the Reichstag as early as December 1914. Between Liebknecht and Luxemburg there were certain nuances. Liebknecht wanted a mass party of workers; Luxemburg clung to the intellectual purity of the Spartakusbund. Liebknecht was fired by the Russian example and would readily have embraced the Russian alliance. Luxemburg had long ago qualified her admiration for Lenin and the Bolsheviks; the programme which she drafted for the young German party contained no reference to the

Russians, and only one — as an inconspicuous afterthought — to the international solidarity of the workers. Radek, who brought greetings from the Russian Communist Party and addressed the founding congress at enormous length on the affinities between the Russian and German revolutions, was apparently heard without much enthusiasm. But these initial difficulties were soon eclipsed by a major tragedy. In the middle of January 1919, after a period of spasmodic street fighting in Berlin, Liebknecht and Luxemburg were arrested by the police and murdered by nationalist thugs "while trying to escape."

The inauspicious character of these beginnings dogged the whole history of the German Communist Party. During its first two years, it remained a small, divided and persecuted faction without any mass following or any influence on affairs. In the autumn of 1920, a formal split was brought about in the much divided Independent Social-Democratic Party, and a majority of the rank and file joined the German Communist Party, giving it for the first time some claim to regard itself as a workers' party. Later, under the stress of economic disaster, its numbers grew and at certain moments it appeared to threaten the already tottering and unstable structure of the Weimar republic. But its strength and influence were never anything like as great as was pretended by those — Germans and others — who used German Communism as a bogey. One of the first of these was Colonel House, Woodrow Wilson's mentor, who before the end of October 1918 had already drawn the attention of Clemenceau and Lloyd-George to "the danger of bringing about a state of Bolshevism in Germany if the terms of the armistice are

made too stiff." "If vindictiveness prevails," wrote
Walther Rathenau in an open letter to the victorious
Allies in December 1918, " then one of the formerly strongest props in the European structure will be destroyed, and
the boundary of Asia will advance to the Rhine." Lloyd
George himself took up the same cue in his confidential
memorandum of March 26, 1919, which was designed to
persuade Clemenceau of the necessity of moderation in
the demands to be made on Germany in the peace treaty.
" The greatest danger that I see in the present situation,"
he wrote, " is that Germany may throw in her lot with
Bolshevism and place her resources, her brains, her vast
organizing power at the disposal of the revolutionary
fanatics whose dream it is to conquer the world for
Bolshevism by force of arms ": all this would happen " if
Germany goes over to the Spartakists." The fear of
Communism in Germany was invoked by every German
statesman of the Weimar republic who had to deal with
the western Allies, down to and including Stresemann, long
before Hitler gave it the central place in Nazi propaganda.
Throughout the period betwen the two world wars the
bogey of Bolshevism played a far more significant role in
German history than anything ever achieved or attempted
by the German Communist Party.

The fears on which Lloyd George had played in 1919
of a coming together of Germany and Russia were well
founded, and were keenly felt by all the peacemakers in
Paris. But the bogey of German Communism served to
mask the real source from which the danger came. The
sham revolution of November 1918 had put the Social-
Democrats into the seats of government, and had led to

the creation of an embryonic German Communist Party. But, behind this pretense of a violent swing to the Left, it had left untouched the real foundations of the social and political order. The Hohenzollern monarchy in its last years had provided a solemn facade for the rule of the General Staff and of big industry; these two forces maintained a firm alliance, into which the East Prussian Junkers entered as a subsidiary and no longer quite independent unit. The Weimar republic provided a different facade, less dignified but better adapted to the exigencies of the time, for the rule of the same forces. At the end of 1918 Germany lay prostrate and helpless. Her recovery would depend on the rapidity with which these two forces could regain their equilibrium and their authority. The policy of the new Germany would depend on their calculation of where their interest lay. Here, and not among the more vocal parties of the Left, were the factors which would prove decisive for German-Soviet relations under the Weimar republic.

While the German armies at the front were in full retreat and disintegration, what was left of the German high command did some quick thinking. On November 10, 1918, an agreement was made between Hindenburg and Ebert, the Social-Democratic president of the Council of People's Commissars. The army would support a Social-Democratic regime to the extent of maintaining order in its name and upholding its authority: the tacit counterpart was that the government would support the army and do nothing to undermine its interests.[1] For the next three months the

---

[1] The details of the agreement, which was concluded by telephone between Berlin and army headquarters, as well as the extent of Hindenburg's and

reestablishment of order as the army understood it was
the sole preoccupation in military circles. There is, however, a record of a more general discussion at staff headquarters in Berlin on December 20, 1918: Major Kurt
von Schleicher expressed the view that Germany's political
recovery depended on her economic recovery, and General
Hans von Seeckt, just back from his appointment as
German adviser to the Turkish General Staff, retorted that
it depended on making Germany once more " eligible to
conclude an alliance " (bundnisfähig). The discussion was
not pursued. But in such a context and in the mouth of
a soldier the word " alliance " could spell only Russia. On
March 15, 1919, a decree was issued creating a new
German army, the Reichswehr, on a basis of voluntary
recruitment. The building up of the Reichswehr, in which
both Seeckt and Schleicher played an important part, was
the first step to a revival of Germany's military strength.
Seeckt occupied the crucial post of chief of staff to the
eastern command in East Prussia.

The other great power in Germany had been equally
stunned by the disaster, but reacted to it with equal
promptness. On November 15, 1918, five days after the
Hindenburg-Ebert agreement, Stinnes, the greatest captain
of industry, came to terms with Legien, the patriotic trade
union leader. Industry, instead of fighting the unions as
in the past, would recognize and support their exclusive
authority in labour matters; the unrecorded counterpart
was that the trade unions on their part would do nothing
to assail the fundamental interests of industry. The agree-

Ebert's personal responsibility for it, are still matters of controversy; but
the fact of its conclusion and its general purport are not in dispute.

ment was reached at a moment when the industrialists, like the army, seemed hopelessly discredited, and the trade unions were at the height of their power and prestige. Nevertheless it worked primarily to the advantage of the industrialists. Shortly afterwards another significant development occurred — the foundation on February 3, 1919, of a comprehensive General Union of German Industry (*Reichsverband der Deutschen Industrie*). Before 1914 significant divisions of interest had existed between different sectors of German industry, between heavy and light industry, between industry working for the home and for the export market, between industry working for western and for eastern export markets. These differences were now being gradually wiped out. The war had helped to weld the organization of German industry into a single whole; the growth of vertical trusts was just beginning to combine heavy and light industry into composite entities; and the widely advertised decision of the victorious Allies to exclude German exports from western markets impelled the whole of German industry to face east. All these interests were represented in the new Union of German Industry which signalized the predominance of heavy industry, notably in the person of Stinnes, in German industrial policy. The interests of German heavy industry lay, at home, in large-scale constructional works and, preferably, in armaments; abroad, in access to the markets of the industrially undeveloped countries of eastern Europe and Asia.

The German attitude to Russia resulting from these conditions in the summer of 1919 was ably summed up in a contemporary British report from Berlin:

All classes in Germany are looking towards Russia for one reason or another. The extremists of the Left look upon her as the realization of their own political ideals; the pan-Germans look upon her as providing the only possible outlet for surplus population and compensation for the loss of colonies. Officers think that she may provide employment, which is no longer possible in their own country. Industrialists think that she will provide employment for capital and ultimately be the means of paying off the war indemnity. The realization of these ideas, however, lies in the far future, and, for the present, communication is much too difficult to make any practical steps possible.

In the Germany of 1919 all roads led to Russia, all the roads that mattered, all the roads that were open. But they were long roads to a distant goal, and the strength to travel along them was not yet very great. The first impulse came from events in the Baltic — the great land and sea bridge between Germany and Russia, the point where Germans have advanced towards Russia and Russians pushed forward their outposts towards Germany, where the territorial and human barrier between the two great nations is at its thinnest and least substantial. Here and only here the German armies did not disintegrate in the hour of defeat, maintaining their cohesion as a disciplined fighting force under the command of General von der Goltz. For this the Allies themselves were partly responsible. They were haunted by two fears — the fear of Russian Bolshevism sweeping westward over Germany and the fear of a junction between Germany and Russia. In November 1918 the first fear predominated over the second. Article XII of the armistice bound Germany to evacuate all territories formerly belonging to the Russian Empire " as soon as the Allies shall think the moment suitable, having regard to the internal situation of those territories." It was intimated that the moment for the evacuation of the Baltic had not yet come; and the German troops gratefully dug themselves in.

Six months later the situation had changed. Germany seemed to have steadied herself and the Bolshevik danger was less imminent. British policy in the Baltic swung over to the new design of building up small independent states in Estonia, Latvia and Lithuania which, together with Poland, would constitute a solid barrier to keep Germany and Russia apart. To this design Von der Goltz was a serious obstacle. On May 3, 1919, the Allied armistice commission was instructed to inform the German armistice commission that the time had come to recall Von der Goltz and his army. When nothing happened, a formal order was given to the German Government on June 18 to withdraw and disband the German armies in the Baltic.

But by this time the order was easier to give than to enforce. General von der Goltz was now at the head of a powerful and well-disciplined army. He had been reinforced by a strong Landeswehr recruited from the large colonies of German settlers in the Baltic, who wholeheartedly shared his ambition to overthrow the Bolsheviks and restore the Russian Empire and were bitterly opposed to any plan for the establishment of independent Baltic states. He had attracted to his side several more or less organized " white " Russian units eager to participate in the anti-Bolshevik crusade. Most important of all, he had become the rallying point and the symbol of all those elements in Germany itself which were opposed to the new regime in Germany and to the policy of compromise with it practised by the High Command. The call was

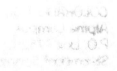

clear and compelling. Von der Goltz was fighting Germany's enemies in the east while the German Government at Versailles was making its cowardly submission to Germany's enemies in the west. Von der Goltz stood, for the first time since Germany's defeat, for a bold and independent foreign policy — to overthrow the Bolsheviks, to restore monarchy in Russia and then, in alliance with a reconstituted Russia, to defy the west. It was a fantastic design, but in 1919 it appealed to many German hearts. As Von der Goltz afterwards explained, " our whole policy stands and falls by the Russian-German bridge "; and one of his subordinates added that the British in enforcing his withdrawal were merely trying to " steal from Germany the opportunity of having before long a great and powerful ally — Russia." Throughout the summer and autumn of 1919 thousands of disbanded German soldiers were recruited in Berlin and despatched, more or less openly, to swell the German army in the Baltic; and released Russian prisoners of war were sent to the same destination.

For three months Von der Goltz defied the efforts of the allies to get him out. While the Social-Democratic government in Berlin was perhaps sincere in its desire to comply with the Allied demand, the Social-Democratic Reichskommissar for East Prussia, Winnig by name, worked hand in glove with the eastern armies. On the other hand, Major Tschunke, an officer on Seeckt's staff posted at Kovno in the autumn of 1919, reported at that time that the operations in the Baltic were creating not a bridge, but a wall, " between us and the Russians "; and Seeckt came round to this opinion. It is clear that the new headquarters staff of the Reischswehr was anxious to wind up the Baltic adventure and threw what influence it had into the scales against it. When Von der Goltz was at length compelled to withdraw, half his army turned itself into volunteers and took service with some "white" Russian formations under an adventurer of Caucasian origin calling himself Count Avalov-Bermondt, who carried on the war against the Bolsheviks for several months longer. Since the troops could no longer be paid from government sources, the financing of Avalov-Bermondt was taken over by an "Anti-Bolshevik League," whose large resources came from the well-filled coffers of the newly created General Union of German Industry.

The ambition of the German extreme Right to build a bridge to Russia by overthrowing the Bolsheviks and creating a German-Russian alliance with a restored Russian monarchy was as remote from reality as the ambition of the German extreme Left to build a bridge to Russia by overthrowing the bourgeois German Government and creating a German-Russian alliance on the basis of a common proletarian revolution. What occurred at this time to hardly anyone on the German side, and to nobody at all on the Allied side, was that a Russian-German alliance could be hoped for, or feared, in any other form. Both sides were mesmerized by the ideological issue. The German Right might overthrow the Bolsheviks and enter into an alliance with a restored Right in Russia; the German Left might make a revolution in Germany and enter into an alliance with the Russian Left in the person of the Bolsheviks. But it seemed unthinkable that the German Right should enter into an alliance with the Russian Left. This over-estimate of the ideological factor was very persistent, especially in the western camp. As late as 1925, with the evidence of Rapallo before his eyes, the British Ambassador in Berlin still clung to the belief that "prolonged cooperation between the German Right and the Russian Left is unthinkable." In 1919 only one episode spoke in the opposite sense; and this episode passed unnoticed by the Allies, was apparently not reported to Moscow, and was known only to a handful of people in Berlin. Yet it contained the germ of the whole history of German-Soviet relations for the next three years, and indeed much later. It is one of the most curious and illuminating episodes of recent history.

After the killing of Liebknecht and Luxemburg, the German police spread their net for other Communist leaders, and early in February 1919 arrested Radek, who had been the delegate of the Russian party at the founding congress of the German Communist Party. He was lodged in the Moabit prison in the Lehrterstrasse and put, according to his own account, into "heavy irons." A prolonged interrogation followed, during which Radek was kept in close confinement. What authority intervened in his favor can only be guessed. But on the completion of the interrogation, apparently in August 1919,[2] the Ministry of War took charge of him and transferred him to a privileged room where, for two months, he occupied a position mid-way between that of a prisoner and of an honoured guest. In Radek's own words he established a "political salon." Passes to visit him

[2] The only indication of the date given by Radek for his transfer to the privileged room is that "the heroic Hungarian revolution had already been crushed." This happened in the first days of August 1919.

were obtained from the Ministry of War. In Octobeɪ 1919 he was released from prison and allowed to move into the private apartment first of a retired general, and later of a police commissioner; and early in December he returned to Moscow. During this period he saw all the leading German Communists and played an active part in the affairs of the German Communist Party; one young Communist from Vienna who visited him frequently describes herself as receiving from him " a whole course in Communism." He received many of the leaders of the Independent Social-Democratic Party, including Hilferding, and a few members of the Social-Democratic Party. The famous German journalist, Maximilien Harden, induced Radek to write an article for his journal *Die Zukunft*. Another visitor was an English radical journalist, Philips Price, to whom he discoursed on world revolution.

Radek's most interesting and important contacts were however, not those with the Left, and it was hardly for the sake of these that military authority treated him with so much indulgence. Among his earliest visitors were the former Turkish Prime Minister and Minister for War, Talaat and Enver. The occasion was piquant. It was a little over a year since Talaat had confronted Radek across the table at Brest-Litovsk as the plenipotentiary of a victorious power. Radek propounded to the Turks a project for an alliance between Russian Bolshevism and Turkish nationalism against British and western imperialism; the novelty and audacity of this project can be measured by reflecting how whole-heartedly the Bolsheviks were at this time committed to the encouragement of Communist revolution — in Turkey as well as anywhere

else. Radek advised his visitors to proceed to Moscow
to discuss the matter — a course which they eventually
followed. Radek had, however, other military visitors. The
most persistent of these was a General von Reibnitz,[3] a
former associate of Ludendorff, from whose rabid anti-
Bolshevik views, however, he now strongly dissented. He
had studied Lenin, and advocated " not only alliance with
Soviet Russia, but a so-called peaceful revolution." Radek
described him a little contemptuously as " the first representative of the species known as ' national Bolsheviks '
with whom I had to deal."

A more serious impression was made by the visit of
Walther Rathenau, who was the son of the founder of the
big German electrical combine, the A. E. G., and the creator in the first world war of the Raw Materials Division of
the German Ministry of War — the counterpart and fore-
runner of the British and French ministries of munitions.
His Jewish race, his keen and inquisitive mind and his
unstable temperament made him a non-typical representative whether of German industry or of German bureau-
cracy; but he had his foot in both these camps. Radek not
unfairly detected in him " a great abstract intelligence,
an absence of any intuition, and a morbid vanity." Though
the open letter to the Allies already quoted expressed a
genuine horror of Bolshevism, the Russian revolution had
a strong intellectual fascination for Rathenau. As early as
April 1919 he sent a " reliable young man " to Russia to
" gather information about Lenin's system "; and he was
a prime mover in the setting up at the beginning of 1920

[3] Radek, writing seven years later, calls him Raivnitz in one place and
Reignitz in another.

by a small group of industrialists of a " study commission " for Russia. He now came to Radek without any preliminaries, settled himself comfortably one leg crossed over the other, and for more than an hour " developed his view of the world situation." He admitted that there could be no return to capitalism and claimed to have propounded in his writings a " constructive socialism " — the first scientific step in advance of Marx, who had given only " a theory of destruction." The workers might destroy; but for construction the leadership of " the spiritual aristocracy " would be required. There would be no revolution in Germany for long years, since the German worker was " a philistine." Reverting to Russia, Rathenau added: " Probably in a few years' time I shall come to you as a technician and you will receive me in silken garments." Radek deprecated the idea that Bolsheviks would ever wear silken garments. But the pregnant offer of the services of German technicians started new trains of thought. The habit of looking east had set in fast among German industrialists.

After Radek left the prison in October, the stream of visitors continued. He saw the leaders of the German Communist Party, Paul Levi and Klara Zetkin, who had feared to compromise themselves by visiting him in the prison. Rathenau came again, bringing with him Felix Deutsch, the general manager of A. E. G. But Deutsch, who was married to the daughter of an American banker, expressed greater faith than Rathenau in the prospects of capitalism, and the conversation seems to have had no result. Among Radek's new visitors two were of special importance. Colonel Max Bauer, Ludendorff's former chief of intelli-

gence, looked forward to the seizure of power in Germany
by the Right, or specifically by the army, but not until
" the workers are disillusioned with bourgeois democracy
and come to the conclusion that a ' dictatorship of labour '
is possible in Germany only by agreement between the
working class and the officer class." Radek records: " He
gave me to understand that on this basis the officers might
strike a bargain with the Communist Party and with
Soviet Russia; they understand that we cannot be conquered and that we are Germany's allies in the struggle
with the Entente." Admiral Hintze, once German naval
attaché in Petersburg and Minister for Foreign Affairs for
a brief period in the summer of 1918, during which he
signed a series of agreements with Russia supplementary
to Brest-Litovsk, now " stood for a deal with Soviet
Russia," and asked Radek whether world revolution would
come in the west " in time to prevent the Entente strangling Germany." It was one of Radek's few visitors from
the Social-Democratic Party, Heilmann by name, who ex-
posed the reverse side of the medal and insisted that
Germany had a western as well as an eastern destiny;
since " German industry is without raw material and the
country without bread," there was nothing for it but submission to the dictates of American capital. It was a
topsy-turvy world in which the German Right toyed with
Bolshevism and world revolution, and German Social-
Democrats looked for salvation to American capitalism.

The German attitude towards Russia and towards
Bolshevism in the autumn of 1919 was still utterly con-
fused. But as more and more practical issues had to be
solved certain lines began to appear in sharp relief. The

Communist Left continued to believe that a communist revolution and alliance with Russia were inseparable aspects of one policy, and was doomed to sterility through failing to make any distinction between them. The same failure was equally fatal to those groups of the extreme Right represented by Ludendorff, Von der Goltz and many others, who believed that the overthrow of Bolshevism and the restoration of the monarchy in Russia was the necessary condition of a German-Russian alliance. Other groups of the Right, of whom Reibnitz and Bauer were typical, were moving towards a conception of an alliance with Russia which was indeed conditional on some kind of German revolution, but on a revolution which would keep the army in its commanding position. These ideas were in themselves fantastic; but from them it was a comparatively short step to the idea that the Russian alliance could be secured without any revolution in Germany at all. The taking of this step was a gradual process. It was associated with the name of Seeckt, the creator of the new Reichswehr, the advocate of a working compromise between the army and the Social-Democratic regime, the stern critic of any policy of adventure, and the strongest military opponent of the anti-Bolshevik line of Ludendorff and Von der Goltz. No evidence exists of any contact at this time between Seeckt and Radek. But Seeckt, as a friend and associate of Enver in his Turkish days, may well have been cognisant of Enver's conversation with Radek; and Radek specifically records that Enver " was the first to explain to German military men that Soviet Russia is a new and growing world Power with which they must count if they really want to fight against the Entente." The notion of a potential alliance between German nationalism and Russian Bolshevism must certainly have been planted at this time in Seeckt's receptive mind, however fantastic and unrealizable such a project may have seemed for the immediate future. Since an understanding with Russia remained " a permanent aim of German policy," he wrote to a military colleague shortly afterwards, it was " inappropriate to antagonize Russia's masters." It was a significant moment when in November 1919 he was appointed head of the so-called Truppenamt in the German Ministry of War — the camouflaged form of the general staff which had been prohibited by the Versailles Treaty. For the next four years German policy towards Russia was to be the policy of Seeckt.

On the Russian side the picture at this time is far simpler. Exactly how far Radek went in his conversations with his German visitors is not known. But his conclusion was clearly and unequivocally recorded in a pamphlet written before his departure from Germany at the beginning of December 1919. " The problem of the foreign policy of Soviet Russia," he announced, " . . . consists in attaining a *modus vivendi* with the capitalist states." And in his article for *Die Zukunft*, which was addressed to " right-minded bourgeois," he proclaimed that " Germany and Russia need economic relations with one another because neither country can hope to get from the Entente alone what it needs and because they can help one another in many ways." But nobody in Russia was yet thinking on these lines. Nobody but Radek in the Russian Communist Party was sufficiently well informed or sufficiently detached to think in any other terms than those of an early

German revolution. Communication between Moscow and Berlin during the whole of 1919 was virtually non-existent. Radek had no opportunity either to make reports to the Kremlin or to receive instructions. When he returned to Moscow in December 1919, his conception of a Russian-German alliance in the form of a *modus vivendi* between Communism and capitalism met with no sympathy or understanding. The civil war, still in a critical state, was the all-absorbing preoccupation of the Bolshevik leaders; nothing short of a world-wide proletarian revolution could — it seemed — put an end to Allied aid to the " whites." Thus, while Radek at the end of 1919 had formed a clearer idea of what the future held in store than anyone else, this idea made slower progress in Soviet Russia than in Germany. Soviet foreign policy flowed for the present in quite different channels.

Chapter II

RUSSIA, GERMANY AND WORLD REVOLUTION

OF ALL COUNTRIES in the world, Germany was the one which the Bolsheviks found it most difficult to approach realistically and empirically: they saw it from the outset, and long continued to see it, through a haze of ideological preconceptions. Germany was, from the Marxist standpoint, the most advanced capitalist country — most advanced, not only in efficiency, but in organization and structure. It was the country where industrial capital was concentrated in the fewest hands; Hilferding, the leading economic thinker among the German Social-Democrats, had written before the war that it would suffice to take over the six largest Berlin banks in order to control the whole of German industry. It was the country where the planned direction of the economy had made the smoothest and most rapid strides in the first world war. Germany was, therefore, the country most surely ripe for a socialist revolution. It seemed almost a freak that this revolution should have broken out first in backward Russia. After the October revolution had taken place, Lenin insisted more strongly than ever that the European revolution, and more specifically the German revolution, could be only just round the corner; he refused to believe that it could be delayed for more than a few weeks or months or that the Russian revolution could long survive without it. The Bolshevik regime almost went under at the beginning of 1918 by staking everything at Brest-Litovsk on the conviction that the German revolution was imminent. Bolshevik jubilation when the German revolution actually started in November 1918 has already been described. Even when it ended in disappointment and the German Soviets were rejected in favour of the parliamentary constitution of the Weimar republic, Bolshevik hopes were not dashed. The events of November 1918 were diagnosed in retrospect as the German " February " revolution which had overthrown the Kaiser just as the Russian February revolution had overthrown the Tsar; the German " October " revolution could not now be far behind.

This mood of revolutionary optimism was maintained throughout 1919 and helped the Bolshevik regime to survive the darkest days of the civil war. The Communist International (Comintern for short) was founded in Moscow in March 1919, though the only German delegate who got through came with a mandate to oppose the immediate foundation of a new International, and was induced to abstain from voting only in order not to mar the formal unanimity of the decision. There was no thought at this time of distinguishing between the revolutionary policy of Comintern and the foreign policy of the Soviet state as administered by the People's Commissariat of Foreign Affairs (Narkomindel). Chicherin, the People's Commissar for Foreign Affairs, figured prominently at the first congress of Comintern and on its executive committee. When the terms of the Versailles treaty were announced, Chicherin signed an appeal to the German workers, which was issued in German by Comintern, urging them to join the ranks of the " revolutionary communist fighters " as the sole means of " salvation from your present calamity." Surrounded by civil war and cut off from regular contacts with the outside world, the Soviet Government was unlikely to abandon its hopes of world revolution or its use of revolutionary propaganda as its one effective weapon. It believed implicitly in the coming German revolution because it could find no other way of believing in its own future. This was true in the economic as well as in the military sense. Lenin's famous remark that, by a queer trick of history, socialism had been realized in our day in two separate halves — the economic half in Germany, the political half in Russia — carried with it the implication that what was required to usher in a full socialist society was to reunite the two halves by bringing the political revolution to Germany.

Thus in the winter of 1919-1920, when the civil war at length took a decisive turn in favour of the Bolsheviks, there was an acute contrast between the optimism of Moscow and the pessimism of the small and discouraged German Communist Party. In March 1920, a few days after Comintern had celebrated its first anniversary and Lenin had proclaimed that " masses of the workers in Germany, England and France are coming over to the side of the Communists," untoward events occurred in Germany. The weak and hesitant German Communist Party had its hand forced — as had happened in January

1919 — by a revolutionary situation which it had done nothing to create and which its leaders secretly deplored. A General named Von Lüttwitz and a civil servant named Kapp organized a revolt — the so-called Kapp *putsch* — against the Social-Democratic government in Berlin. Some of the military units which carried out the *putsch*, such as the famous Erhardt brigade, had participated in the fighting in the Baltic and had never been disbanded; others were composed of nationalist soldiers or adventurers of a similar type who returned to the colours to fight against the Weimar democracy. On March 13, 1920, the ministers fled from Berlin to Stuttgart, and a Right nationalist government under Kapp was proclaimed in Berlin. Its weakness was, however, quickly revealed. The Reichswehr remained passive. It was unthinkable that German soldiers should fire on their former comrades; but, while the insurgents enjoyed the sympathy of generals of the old school like Ludendorff and Von der Goltz, Seeckt and the new general staff — the men who had already brought Von der Goltz's Baltic venture to an end — made clear their opposition to the insurrection, while the German People's Party, which had been organized in 1919 under the leadership of Stresemann as the party of large-scale industry and commerce, came out with a strong declaration against Kapp and in defence of constitutional government. The coup might still have succeeded but for a general strike called by the trade unions, which prevented the new authority from establishing itself and in the end forced a restoration of the old government. When the strike was declared, the German Communist Party headquarters in Berlin had officially announced that the time was not

yet ripe for action — an attitude which was afterwards
excused, and could only be excused, by invoking the
numerical weakness of the party. In private the leaders
denounced the strike, whose organizer, the trade union
leader Legien, had more than once been singled out for
attack by Lenin as a typical " social-patriot," and loftily
treated the struggle between the Social-Democrats and
the nationalists as a matter of indifference to Communists
who were equally hostile to both. Only on the second day,
when the rank and file of the party were to be found
following the lead of their trade union comrades, did the
party line change to one of rather half-hearted support of
the strike. But local action by Communists went much
further than this, especially in Saxony and in the Ruhr,
where Social-Democrats and Communists took joint action
against the nationalists; in Saxony they even united to
form a Soviet government which abdicated only when the
putsch had been finally defeated. But, once the danger
was over, the will of the Left parties failed them. A
coalition government with the Centre was once more
formed. The real victors of March 1920 were the Reichswehr, and the reprisals which followed fell not to much on
the authors of the *putsch* as on the workers who had come
out against it. The victory of the Reichswehr was crowned
by the appointment of Seeckt, hitherto head of the
Truppenamt, as its commander-in-chief: " chief of the
army command " was his official title.

The Kapp *putsch* was a significant landmark, and
several instructive lessons could be drawn from it. The
weakness of the German Communist Party was plainly
demonstrated, and its members shown as hesitating

between an attitude which treated nationalists and Social-Democrats equally as agents of bourgeois capitalism and refused to distinguish between them — this was the official party line — and an attitude which leaned towards a defensive alliance with the Social-Democrats against the common nationalist enemy — this was the inclination of many of the rank and file. A similar pattern was to repeat itself in the last days of the Weimar republic. The Social-Democratic Party had reacted to the Kapp *putsch* in a vigorous and organized way through the trade unions by using the workers' traditional weapon of resistance — the strike. But it had no positive plan of action; not only did it lack any ambition to seize power by revolutionary means, but it shrank from the exercise of power when power was thrust into its hands. The events of March 1920 confirmed the main lesson of November 1918: the incapacity of the largest and best organized German political party to rule the country. As regards the Right, the Kapp *putsch* had brought to an issue — and this is its great importance in the history of German-Soviet relations — the struggle between the two elements in the German army. A nice distinction is said to have been drawn on one occasion by Blomberg, later Hitler's Field-Marshal: " It was a point of honour with the Prussian officer to be correct; it is a duty of the German officer to be crafty." It was the old Prussian tradition which fought its last battles in the Baltic, rejected the Weimar republic root and branch, and made its last serious bid for power in the Kapp *putsch*: the " correct " Prussian generals had learned nothing and forgotten nothing. The new Reichswehr and its camouflaged general staff, in the person of men like

General von Seeckt and Major von Schleicher, enjoying the support of industry, accepted the Weimar republic as a convenient facade of government, behind which German military power could be re-built by all means, licit and illicit; the Kapp *putsch* was the victory of this new German " craftiness " over what was left of the old Prussian tradition. In terms of Soviet-German relations, it was the victory of men who believed that the traditional German-Russian alliance could be reconstituted by way of an agreement with the Bolsheviks over men who believed that the overthrow of the Bolsheviks was the only road to the reconstruction of the German-Russian alliance and therefore a primary aim of German policy.

In Moscow nothing of all this was understood in the spring of 1920. The diagnosis of the Kapp *putsch* seemed simplicity itself. In August 1917 a Tsarist general named Kornilov had attempted a coup against the Provisional Government which repulsed it without much difficulty. The Kapp *putsch* was the " German Kornilov affair." The German revolutionary calendar had moved slowly but surely from February to August; the approach of October was only the more certain and inexorable. Belief in the existence of general rules governing the revolutionary process, and consequently in a parallelism between revolutions in different countries, was inherent in Marxism. But the confident and dogmatic application of this belief at a time when the Bolshevik leaders had few sources of information and fewer direct contacts to bring home to them the realities of the political situation, and in particular of Left parties and movements, in Germany and other western countries, bred many illusions. It was rash to assume a close and unassailable analogy between the revolutionary time-table in Russia, which had made an almost direct transition from autocracy to the proletarian revolution, and in countries where the proletariat had undergone a long period of indoctrination in the theory and practice of the bourgeois state. The Bolsheviks constantly underestimated the proportion of German workers who had derived benefits from trade union and parliamentary procedures and could not easily be weaned from belief in the validity of these procedures. Lenin never really understood why " reformism," which meant nothing in Russia, was a persistent and dangerous rival to revolutionary Marxism in the German Social-Democratic Party, and why illegal action, which was accepted as a matter of course by Russian workers, aroused strong prejudices among many German workers. The embarrassment became acute over the question of the relation between party leadership and the masses. In Russia what was necessary was to create a revolutionary consciousness among masses of hitherto politically unconscious workers; and for this purpose the imprint of a strong and absolute revolutionary leadership was a paramount need. But the same conception was not applicable, or applicable only with far-reaching qualifications, to a country like Germany, where the problem was not to imprint a revolutionary consciousness on the *tabula rasa* of politically unconscious masses, but to penetrate and transform a political consciousness already highly developed in a trade union and parliamentary tradition. This task was different from anything that confronted the Russian Bolsheviks, and was far more subtle and complicated; and the misunderstanding of this difference explains why the prescriptions offered to the German Communist Party by the Bolsheviks, and afterwards by Comintern, were so often inappropriate, and why the Bolshevik diagnosis of the German political situation was so often radically at fault.

Russian optimism about the prospects of European revolution soon received a strong reinforcement. In the middle of May 1920, when the civil war seemed over, Pilsudski launched an attack on Soviet Russia and Polish troops penetrated the Ukraine as far as Kiev. But the Red Army struck back quickly and, by the middle of July, was driving the routed Polish troops before it towards Warsaw. It was at this moment that the Communist International opened its second congress in Moscow. A large map of Europe hung in the congress hall; and on it were marked day by day the advances made by the Red Army in its triumphant march to the west. Faith in the impending German and European revolution seemed just about to be justified. Many in western Europe as well as in Moscow believed that Poland's doom was sealed and that the revolution would flow on westwards over Germany. But in August, when the congress had already dispersed, a sudden reversal occurred in the fortunes of war. The Red Army sustained a dramatic defeat before Warsaw, and retired as rapidly as it had advanced. The retreat continued into Russian territory, where an armistice was accepted in October. Revolutionary ardour cooled, and was succeeded in Moscow by a mood of sober reflexion.

It would be an anachronism to speak at this time of any divergence between the revolutionary and the national aspects of Russian policy, between the aims and purposes of Comintern and those of Narkomindel. But the Polish war of the summer of 1920 had a profound effect, direct and indirect, on German-Russian relations. In those relations Poland had always been a sensitive spot. For a century and a half after the first partition of Poland, the Polish question had remained acute with an intermittent threat of intervention from western Europe on behalf of the Poles; and, as long as this continued, a common German-Russian interest in the suppression of Polish liberties and in the exclusion of the western Powers from eastern Europe held Germany and Russia together. But, after the failure of the last great Polish insurrection in 1863, the Polish question ceased to exist, and seemed to have been erased from the public consciousness of Europe; and the removal of this threat was one of the factors which, after Bismarck's downfall, allowed Germany and Russia to drift apart. The war of 1914 at once brought back the Polish question to life. The unlooked-for simultaneous collapse of both Russia and Germany at the end of the war automatically restored Poland to a position of predominance in eastern Europe which she had not occupied since the 17th century. Poland became an outpost of the western allies, and the main eastern bastion of the Versailles Treaty. Poland's territorial acquisitions in 1919 at the expense of Germany made Germany her lasting enemy. Eastward she also advanced some distance into Russian territory. But the extent of her ambitions at Russia's expense were not revealed till Pilsudski invaded the Ukraine in May 1920. Taking a long view, it may be said that Pilsudski's action sealed the fate of Poland; for it is a consequence of Poland's geographical situation that

she cannot afford for long to be on bad terms simultaneously with both her great neighbours.

The Polish offensive against Soviet Russia in May 1920
did not kindle any very lively German interest in the war.
But when the Red Army unexpectedly struck back and,
early in July, began a triumphant march into Poland,
excitement in Germany became intense. Germany's principal enemy in the east was in mortal danger, the overthrow of the eastern bastion of Versailles at the hands of
Russia seemed imminent. The Allied Powers drew the
same conclusion, and hastily organized the despatch of aid
to Poland in the form of military advisers and supplies of
munitions. Germany replied with a declaration of neutrality which involved a ban on the transit of munitions
through Germany to Poland. In the Free City of Danzig,
formerly German and now under Allied administration, the
German dockers went on strike and refused to handle
munitions shipped to Poland through that port. German
volunteers (Tukhachevsky, the Red Army commander,
speaks of " hundreds and thousands " of them) flocked to
join the Red Army — a curious reversal of the situation
of the previous autumn, when German volunteers were
flocking to the Baltic to fight the Bolsheviks. The German
Communist newspaper *Rote Fahne* adoped so militant an
attitude in advocating a German alliance with Soviet
Russia that it incurred the accusation from other Left
parties of trying to involve the German workers in a war
with France.

German sympathy did not pass unnoticed in the Soviet
camp. Evidence of direct contact is scanty. A contemporary report in the London *Times* of a visit by Trotsky to

East Prussia to negotiate with German staff officers " on political and strategic questions " is certainly false. But there is what appears to be an authentic story of a meeting at Soldau, just inside the East Prussian frontier, between officers and commissars of the Red Army and " German nationalists " at which the Russians boasted that the Red Army would liberate West Prussia, ceded to Poland by the Versailles Treaty, and restore it to the German fatherland. According to Pilsudski's memoirs the Soviet fourth army was so eager to press forward to the Polish Corridor that it lost contact with the other Soviet armies and thus opened a path for Pilsudski's triumphant counter-offensive in front of Warsaw; he quotes the quip of a French officer that " the Soviet fourth army was fighting against the Versailles Treaty rather than against Poland." A curious document of this period is a letter from Enver to Seeckt written from Moscow in ungrammatical German on August 26, 1920. Enver reports that he has just seen " Trotsky's really important *aide* " (this was probably Sklyansky, Deputy Commissar for War), and continues:

There is a party here which has real power, and Trotsky also belongs to this party, which is for an agreement with Germany. This party would be ready to recognize the old German frontier of 1914. And they see only one way out of the present world chaos — that is cooperation with Germany and Turkey. In order to strengthen the position of this party and to win the whole Soviet government for the cause, would it not be possible to give unofficial help, and if possible sell arms? . . . I think it important that you should come to an understanding with their representatives in order that Germany's position also should be clear and certain. To help the Russians one can, in the Corridor or in some suitable place, bring into being a volunteer army or an insurrectionary movement. . . .

If these recommendations could not be put into execution, it may be surmized that the spirit in which they were offered, and Enver's report of opinion in influential circles in Moscow, helped to confirm designs that were already shaping themselves in Seeckt's mind. The proposal to " recognize the old German frontier of 1914," i. e. to support the return to Germany of German territory ceded to Poland under the Versailles Treaty, was not likely to fail of its intended effect. It was inherent in the situation that a bargain could be struck, and could only be struck, at the expense of Poland.

The Polish war had other less direct, but perhaps not less important, repercussions on German-Soviet relations. It brought home to German military leaders for the first time the power of the Red Army as a fighting force and the magnitude of the achievement represented in the creation of that army. Military efficiency has always had a particularly strong appeal to German minds. Max Bauer, Radek's visitor in the autumn of 1919, wrote of Trotsky in his memoirs as " a born military organizer and leader " and added:

How he built up a new army out of nothing in the midst of severe battles and then organized and trained this army is absolutely Napoleonic.

And General Hoffmann in his memoirs passes the same verdict:

Even from a purely military standpoint one is astonished that it was possible for the newly recruited Red troops to crush the forces, at times still strong, of the white generals and to eliminate them entirely.

On the Soviet side, the war against Poland made a patriotic

appeal to countless numbers of the former aristocracy and bourgeoisie and helped bring about a qualified reconciliation between them and the new regime. The civil war had already rallied thousands of former Tsarist officers to the Red Army; more and more now flocked to the colours to fight the Polish invaders, Brusilov, the former Tsarist commander-in-chief, at their head. A British Labour delegation, visiting Russia in the early days of the Polish war, reported " the birth and growth of a new patriotism." Even Zinoviev, the president of Comintern and an enthusiastic protagonist of world revolution, noted that " the war is becoming national," and declared that " we Communists must be at the head of this national movement which will gain the support of the entire population and is growing daily stronger." This new *leitmotif* of national patriotism became after 1920 a permanent ingredient in Soviet foreign policy.

The bleak winter of 1920-1921 finally brought about a change in the attitude of the Bolshevik leaders on many things, world revolution and foreign policy among them. The situation in Russia took an unfavorable turn for the Soviet Government. The civil war had been won; Wrangel, the last of the " white " generals, had capitulated in November. But the peasants, increasingly restive at the constant requisitioning of their grain, broke out in open revolt in more than one province and were everywhere threatening to withhold supplies from the hungry towns. Early in March a serious mutiny occurred in Kronstadt, the fortress at the mouth of the Neva, a few miles from Petrograd, and was quelled with some difficulty. At the congress of the Russian Communist Party in the middle of March 1921

Lenin introduced the measures afterwards known as NEP or the New Economic Policy. The essence of these was the restoration of commercial principles in transactions with the peasants — a partial return, as Lenin admitted, to capitalism; and, while no direct inferences were drawn from this in the field of foreign policy, a compromise with capitalism at home inevitably suggested the possibility of improved relations with capitalist governments abroad. A more conspicuous landmark in this change of front was the conclusion at the same moment — on March 16, 1921 — of the first major international agreement with a capitalist Power, the trade agreement with Great Britain, carrying with it the *de facto* recognition by Great Britain of the Soviet Government. This agreement quickly found imitators. It could hardly fail to stimulate the development of " normal " relations between Soviet Russia and the capitalist countries, and to relegate international revolution to the background as an element of Soviet diplomacy.

These changes were bound to be reflected sooner or later in the Soviet attitude to German-Soviet relations. The defeat of the Red Army in Poland interrupted in the autumn of 1920 the incipient German-Soviet *rapproche-ment*. The victories of the summer seemed in retrospect like· a flash of lightning illuminating a prospect which was now once more shrouded in gloom. But this momentary vision of active collaboration between the two great anti-Versailles powers remained and did its work. Lenin, looking back two months later on these events, recalled that " everyone in Germany, even the blackest reactionaries and monarchists, said that the Bolsheviks would save us, when they saw the Versailles peace splitting at all its seams "; and he noted the presence in Germany of " an unnatural bloc of ' black hundreds ' and Bolsheviks." It was at the All-Russian Congress of Soviets in December 1920 that Lenin for the first time publicly discussed the question of Soviet-German relations in a context other than that of world revolution. Having called Germany " the most advanced country with the exception of America," he went on:

This country, bound by the Versailles treaty, lives in conditions which do not allow it to exist. And in this position Germany is naturally pushed into alliance with Russia. When the Russian armies were approaching Warsaw, all Germany was in a ferment. Alliance with Russia for a country which is strangled, which has the possibility to set in motion gigantic productive forces — all this helped to create political confusion in Germany; the German black hundreds were marching in sympathy with the Russian Bolsheviks and the Spartakists. . . .

Our foreign policy, so long as we are alone and the capitalist world is strong, . . . consists in our being obliged to utilize disagreements. . . . Our existence depends, first, on the existence of a radical split in the camp of the imperialist powers and, secondly, on the fact that the victory of the Entente and the Versailles peace have thrown the vast majority of German nations into a position where they cannot live. . . . The German bourgeois government madly hates the Bolsheviks, but the interests of the international situation are pushing it towards peace with Soviet Russia against its own will.

Thus, three months before the introduction of NEP and the conclusion of the Anglo-Soviet trade agreement, Lenin had hinted in no uncertain terms at the willingness of the Soviet Government to receive German overtures if such should be made. The first step had been taken on the road that led to Rapallo.

There were, however, still obstacles to be overcome. The Soviet Government had never had any objection of principle to enlisting the cooperation of one capitalist country or group of countries against another. Early in 1918, at the time of Brest-Litovsk a tentative enquiry had been made about the possibility of securing allied assistance to continue the war against Germany; later in the year an equally tentative project was mooted to invite German troops into north Russia in order to drive out the allied forces just landed at Murmansk and Archangel. This expedient of driving a wedge between the capitalist Powers and seeking the alliance of one against another was now to become a permanent element in Soviet foreign policy. Yet it was not without its embarrassments. Germany had always occupied a unique place in the Bolshevik scheme of world revolution. It was in Germany that the proletarian revolution had always seemed most imminent and most essential. Soviet policy at this time was far from having achieved the monolithic character attributed to it a later period. Any turn of policy which threatened to interfere with the established programme of world revolution was likely to be strongly resisted in Comintern circles; and the voice of Zinoviev still commanded a large following in the party. It thus happened that, in this same month of March 1921, in which the introduction of the New Economic Policy and the conclusion of the Anglo-Soviet trade agreement pointed the way to a policy of temporary accommodations with the capitalist world, a further attempt was made to stage the drama of the proletarian revolution on the German scene. It was only after the ignominious failure of this attempt that Soviet policy in Germany could be woven into a consistent line.

What came to be known in the history of the German

Communist Party as the " March action " of 1921 was a belated hang-over from the revolutionary enthusiasm generated in the previous summer by the Polish war. Throughout the summer of 1920 the split between Right and Left in the German Independent Social-Democratic Party had been widening. At a party congress in Halle in October 1920, attended by Zinoviev who delivered a long remembered oration lasting four hours, a majority of the party decided to unite with the German Communist Party as a constituent party of the Communist International. This decision at once swelled the members of the German Communist Party from a meagre 50,000 to the respectable figure of 350,000; but the mass infusion of new members rather abruptly changed its character. Hitherto, under the leadership of Paul Levi, a highly cultivated intellectual and a disciple of Rosa Luxemburg, it had carried on the tradition of the Spartakusbund; it remained a centre of intellectual activity and propaganda and looked sceptically at the prospect of immediate revolutionary action. Now it suddenly became a mass party composed predominantly of workers who were unconcerned with the refinements of theory and called for a forward policy. This new demand had the sympathy of Zinoviev who felt himself mainly responsible for the enlargement of the party. But it was opposed by Radek who, as representative of Comintern in Germany, shared Levi's scepticism about German revolutionary prospects and had other ideas about what should be the German policy of the Kremlin. In January 1921 the central committee of the German Communist Party, under Levi's leadership and with Radek's active support, put out an " open letter " to all German parties of the

Left and to the German trade unions appealing to them to join with the German Communist Party in a common campaign for three objects: to improve the lot of the workers by raising wages and controlling prices; to dissolve illegal military formations of the bourgeoisie and to create " organs of proletarian self-defence "; and to establish commercial and diplomatic relations with Soviet Russia. This was not a revolutionary programme and pointed to the creation of what afterwards came to be called a " united front " with parties and organizations which had recently been denounced as traitors to the proletarian cause. Lenin's approval was secured for the " open letter " against the opposition of Zinoviev and Bukharin. But, when it fell completely flat and evoked no response in Germany itself, it had the result of discrediting Levi and encouraging those elements in the German Communist Party which were impatient of Levi's caution and restraint. Levi's fall came, however, on another and extraneous issue. Attending a crucial congress of the Italian party at Leghorn, he took a line opposed to that of the official delegates of Comintern, who denounced his action as a breach of discipline and put forward a demand for a vote of censure against him from the central committee of the German party. Levi had by this time many enemies in the central committee. The vote was carried by a narrow majority; and he and four of his immediate supporters resigned. The vote was generally interpreted in the party as a vote for a more active policy. On March 4, 1921, the day after the vote, the central committee issued an appeal to the German workers to demonstrate in favor of " the overthrow of the German bourgeois government."

At this moment Bela Kun, once the head of the short-lived Hungarian Soviet Government, arrived in Berlin from Moscow as delegate of Comintern with instructions from Zinoviev to galvanize the German party into action. This was in accordance with the line which Zinoviev had taken during the past two or three months. But it may well be, as was afterwards said, that the Kronstadt mutiny and other difficulties at home made Zinoviev particularly insistent on the urgency of creating a diversion in Germany. Bela Kun talked not only to the central committee of the German Party but also to Levi and Klara Zetkin who had just resigned from it: according to Levi, he declared that the party must act and, if necessary, create the provocation for action. In the recriminations which broke out after the failure of the rising, scapegoats had to be found; many later accounts give the impression of a coup planned in Moscow to suit Russian ends and dictated to a reluctant German Communist Party. Two months after the rising a German Communist speaking at a trade union congress in Moscow alleged that " the German Communists let themselves be shot and thrown into prison because they were rendering aid to the Russian proletariat." This picture is somewhat overdrawn. What can fairly be said is that Zinoviev, as president of Comintern, had for some months, against the opposition of Radek, been supporting that section of the German Communist Party which was impatient for action; that Lenin and Trotsky at this time were too much preoccupied with the internal crisis to give any serious attention to German affairs; and that Zinoviev seized the moment of the Kronstadt mutiny to send Bela Kun to Berlin to press his views. Since this coincided

with Levi's resignation, which had given a preponderance of power in the German central committee to the
activists, Zinoviev's recommendations found a ready, even
eager, hearing. But to describe the German March rising
as a considered act of Russian policy carried through a
docile German Communist Party is to read back into 1921
a situation which existed only at a much later period.

The precise course of events which led to the rising is
also controversial. Towards the middle of March disorders
broke out in the Mansfeld mining area of central Germany.
The miners had a reputation of turbulence and many of
them were Communists: whether the disorders were spon-
taneous, or were started at the prompting of the central
committee of the party or of some of its members, has
never been clearly established. On March 16, 1921, the
Reichswehr moved into the area in force and suppressed
the disorders with considerable brutality, carrying out
executions and arrests on a large scale. This was taken
as the " provocation " for which the party had been waiting. On the following day the central committee of the
German Communist Party proclaimed an insurrection
against the government and called on the workers to take
up arms. The organization was mediocre. Desultory
clashes between workers and police or Reichswehr occurred
in many places; only in central Germany where the
trouble had begun was there any serious fighting. A week
later, when the rising had begun to fizzle out, the central
committee announced a general strike. But this only
aggravated the disaster, leading Communist strikers into
fights not only with the police but with the mass of workers
who preferred to stick to their jobs. On March 31, when

the defeat of the Communists was complete with many casualties and thousands of arrests, the central committee called off the whole action.

The collapse of the March rising represented the German angle of the broad change of front in Moscow signalized by the two other major events of March 1921 — the introduction of NEP and the conclusion of the Anglo-Soviet trade agreement. The positive drive towards a temporary accommodation with the capitalist world was accentuated by a new pessimism about the prospects of the European revolution. The attempt of the German Communist Party to take the offensive and carry the day by a frontal attack on the German bourgeois government had ended disastrously and ignominiously; and, where the relatively large and powerful German party had failed, no Communist party in any other country was likely to succeed. The importance of the lessons to be drawn from the March rising was indicated by the length of the discussions devoted to the subject at the third congress of Comintern which met in Moscow in June 1921. Whatever share of responsibility for the rising had been borne by Comintern in general, or Zinoviev in particular, was quietly ignored; the fact that Radek was chosen to make the official report of the subject was significant of the line to be adopted. While the March rising was perfunctorily described as " a step forward," it was treated as a defensive measure forced on the party by the provocative action of the Reichswehr; the party was blamed for not having sufficiently emphasized its defensive character and for having supposed that the moment was ripe for a revolutionary offensive. The atmosphere of the congress re-

flected none of the triumphant enthusiasm of the second
congress a year earlier. Trotsky and Lenin both frankly
registered the change of situation and mood:

Now for the first time [said Trotsky] we see and feel that we are
not so immediately near to the goal, to the conquest of power, to the
world revolution. . . . In 1919 we said to ourselves: "It is a
question of months." Now we say: "It is perhaps a question of
years."

And Lenin added:

It is plain at a glance that, after the conclusion of the peace,
however bad that was, we did not succeed in provoking a revolution
in the capitalist countries. . . . What is essential now is a fundamental
preparation of the revolution and a study of its concrete development
in the principal capitalist countries.

The first practical consequence of this pessimistic diagnosis was the need to win over the masses. It was no
longer sufficient for Communist parties to wrap themselves
in a mantle of doctrinal purity; they must participate
actively as missionaries of Communism in all workers'
organizations. A few months after the congress, the executive committttee of Comintern advocated the formation of
a " united front " for limited common purposes with other
Left parties — a policy which, with many variations and
qualifications, was officially maintained for seven years.
The second consequence was more delicate. If the delay
in the spread of the revolution had now to be reckoned
not in months but in years, then the necessity of a policy
of temporary compromises with the capitalist world, and
in particular with the great capitalist Power of central
Europe, was incontrovertible. After the failure of the
" March action " it was clear that the German revolution
and world revolution would have to wait. The last obstacle
was down. The road to Rapallo was wide open.

Chapter III

THE ROAD TO RAPALLO

THE PROCESS of building up normal state relations between the German bourgeois republic and the Russian Soviet republic was slow and gradual. Towards the end of 1919, shortly before Radek's return to Moscow, a Soviet delegate, Kopp by name, arrived in Berlin. In February 1920 he was officially recognized by the German Government for the limited purpose of negotiating an exchange of prisoners of war; and two agreements on this subject were concluded in the spring of 1920. Later, Kopp's functions were extended to commercial matters, and he came to be accepted as an informal Soviet diplomatic representative in Berlin. In June 1920, Gustav Hilger, a German born in Moscow who had left Russia with the German consular staff in November 1918 and had later worked in Berlin on the repatriation of prisoners of war, reached Moscow as the first unofficial German representative, becoming the German counterpart there of Kopp in Berlin. This tentative stretching out of hands across the ideological barrier was not significant in itself, but promised much for the future. The sudden impetus given to German-Soviet friendship by the Polish war faded away with the retreat of the Red Army and the conclusion of the armistice. It was not till the beginning of 1921, when most Germans became convinced for the first time that the Soviet regime in Russia had come to last, when the lessons of the Polish war had been slowly digested, and when thoughts on the Russian side were beginning to revolve round concepts less far-reaching than world revolution, that the negotiations which led to the Rapallo treaty were first seriously taken in hand. They flowed in three distinct channels — economic, military and political. The economic negotiations proceeded more or less openly, the military and political negotiations in profound secret.

The economic negotiations started first. Economic relations between Germany and Soviet Russia had never been formally severed since peace was concluded at Brest-Litovsk. As early as April 1918, the Soviet Government had established its monopoly of foreign trade, so that all commercial transactions were henceforth conducted with a Soviet department. Trade did not, however, entirely cease. Krasin was in Berlin in the summer of 1918 arranging the shipment of German coal to Russia, and a few cargoes of flax and timber left Petrograd for German or Scandinavian ports. It was the collapse of November 1918 which brought this trickle to a standstill. Throughout 1919 Soviet Russia was completely isolated. After the signature of the Versailles treaty, the Allied Powers even established a " blockade " of Russia (though they refrained from using the word out of consideration for the susceptibilities of international lawyers), and in October 1919 invited Germany to participate in it. Germany refused; and in the Reichstag debate which followed, this decision was applauded, with varying degrees of emphasis, by spokesmen of every party from Left to Right. Though the refusal was put on the characteristic ground that Germany was herself still being subjected to an Allied blockade and that participation presupposed a recognition of equality of rights, it was none the less significant that the first occasion since Versailles on which the German Government had ventured openly and flatly to reject an Allied demand was on a Russian issue. The refusal made no practical difference, since the possibilities of trade did not exist, and Russian isolation continued even after the formal abandonment of the blockade in January 1920. This was the period when foreign traders hesitated to accept Soviet exports for fear that some expropriated former owner, Russian or foreign, of the consignments offered might be able to establish a title to them in the courts, and when even Soviet gold was not accepted at par value on the bullion markets of the world. German firms in general were unwilling, even if they had possessed the means, to take the first plunge into this speculative market, and throughout 1920 German-Soviet trade barely rose above the zero levels of 1919. This cautious mood dominated German official policy. The only concrete reply to Lenin's speech of December 1920 quoted in the previous chapter was a cautious statement by the German Foreign Minister, Simons, in the Reichstag in January 1921 that " Communism is no reason why a republican and bourgeois government should not trade with the Soviet Government." A Communist deputy in the same debate quoted an official report to the effect that Kopp was acting as an intermediary in commercial transactions between the Soviet Government and German firms, and that " this unofficial activity is tolerated so long as the interests and security of the

Reich are not affected." Negotiations were, in fact, going on. Kopp, who came to Moscow from Berlin on leave about this time told *Izvestiya* on February 1, 1921, that there was a prospect of opening trade delegations in the respective capitals in the near future. The German-Soviet trade agreement was, however, not signed till nearly two months after the Anglo-Soviet agreement had set the example and broken the ice. The date was May 6, 1921. It was the day after the Allied governments had sent to Berlin, in the form of an ultimatum, a statement of Germany's total reparations liability and a schedule of payments required by the Allies. The coincidence may have been accidental, or may have been an early instance of a pattern which later became regular in German foreign policy — the playing off of Soviet Russia against the western allies. The most significant clause of the German-Soviet agreement did not concern trade at all; it contained an undertaking by the German Government to deal exclusively with the Soviet Government as the government of Russia, and to have no relations with any " white " émigré organization — the official ending of the anti-Bolshevik crusade. Henceforth, whatever might be the Russian policy of the German Government, it would be directed to maintain relations with the Soviet Government, not to overthrow it. In October 1921 Krestinsky, an old Bolshevik who had formerly been People's Commissar for Finance, was appointed as Soviet representative — not yet a fully accredited diplomatic representative—in Berlin; and a Soviet trade delegation was set up there under Stomonyakov, a Bulgarian who had been Krasin's assistant in London. The corresponding German representative in

Moscow was Wiedenfeld, hitherto head of the foreign trade section of the German Foreign Office.

The importance to Germany of a revival of trade with Soviet Russia was incontestable. Before 1914, Russia had taken 47% of her total imports from Germany, though this figure represented only 8.7% of German exports. Now that German access to western European and oversea markets had been drastically curtailed, the Russian market was of primary importance. That market had, however, shrunk to insignificant dimensions. In 1921, the first year in which Soviet foreign trade became at all active, the total turnover was only one-twelfth of that of 1913; and of the restricted volume of Soviet imports in that year 29% came, thanks to the impulse given by the Anglo-Soviet agreement, from Great Britain and only 25% from Germany. In the latter part of 1921 the opening up of the Russian market became a major preoccupation of German policy. Opinion and interest within German industry were, however, divided on one point. Heavy industry, whose basis was the coal and iron of the Ruhr and of Silesia, was largely independent of imported raw materials and had no important markets in the west. It was therefore free from western affiliations and favoured a direct deal with Soviet Russia. Stinnes was the protoganist of this view among the industrialists, and Stresemann at this time its spokesman in the Reichstag. It was Stresemann who, when Stinnes died two years later, described him as " the strongest power in the economic life of Germany." Light and specialized industries, on the other hand, required oversea imports of raw materials, and found their markets as much in the west and the east; some of them had received American credits or were otherwise linked to American industrial interests. They shared the desire of heavy industry to develop the Russian market, but would have preferred to do it in concert with the west rather than in opposition to it. This sector of German industry was represented politically by the Democratic Party and by Rathenau, who became Minister of Reconstruction in Wirth's government in May 1921; the Franco-German agreement negotiated at Wiesbaden in October 1921 between Rathenau and Loucheur, both industrialists and both politicians in their respective countries, was the first symptom of this new trend. Its ostensible purpose was to solve the reparations problem through a partnership between French and German industry; its more far-reaching aim was to develop this partnership over a much wider field. In December 1921 industrialists and financiers of the Allied countries met in Paris under official patronage to examine a project to establish an industrial consortium for the reconstruction of Europe, whose main function was to be the organization of investment in Russia on an international scale and the exploitation and development of Russian resources and of the Russian market. Rathenau, now no longer a minister but a reparations delegate, had just visited Lloyd George in London and was in Paris during this meeting; and, though he did not officially participate in it, German cooperation was understood to be an essential part of the scheme. This project was part of the preparation for the Genoa conference and was blessed by the Allies at the meeting at Cannes which issued invitations to the conference. Rathenau was at Cannes ostensibly for discussions about reparations; he concluded one of his speeches there with a tactful peroration in which he explained that Germany, though without capital to invest, could contribute to the reconstruction of Europe through her familiarity with " the technical and economic conditions and practices of the east."

These proposals were little to the taste of the Soviet Government. Chicherin warned the world at large that Soviet Russia would accept no project which " took the form of economic domination "; and Lenin declared that any plans for treating Russia as a conquered country were " simple nonsense not worth answering." Radek ingeniously explained that the whole scheme was designed to make Russia help to shoulder the burden of German reparations by taking German goods and supplying raw materials in exchange to the Allies: thus Germany would become an " industrial colony," and Russia an " agrarian colony," of the west. The proposals were regarded with almost equal disfavour by German heavy industry, which wanted direct relations with Soviet Russia without interference from the west. In a debate in the Reichstag in March 1922, the international consortium proposal was vigorously attacked by Stresemann on behalf of the German People's Party. During the winter of 1921-1922, while Rathenau was feeling his way with the Allies, active negotiations were proceeding between German industrialists and the Soviet authorities both for the development of trade and the granting of concessions. The first German-Soviet " mixed companies " — Derutra for transport, Deruluft for air traffic, Derumetall for trade in scrap metal — came into being at this time; all of them involved in one way or another credits from the German concerns involved. Many large German firms were tempted by the offer of concessions in Soviet Russia. A note from Lenin to the Politburo of January 1922 preserved in the Trotsky archives insists on the importance of concluding a concession agreement with Krupp; such agreements were especially valuable on the eve of the Genoa conference, and " particularly with German firms." When therefore the idea of an international consortium collapsed at Genoa, these direct negotiations received a further stimulus. Among the first concessions was the grant to Krupp of a large area on the river Manych, a tributary of the Don, as an experimental farm for the demonstration of tractors and agricultural machinery. In December 1922 it was reported to the foreign affairs committee of the Reichstag that concession agreements had been signed with the Stinnes group and with twenty other German concerns. Comparatively few concessions were in fact granted or taken up. But Soviet trade underwent a considerable expansion; and of an increased volume of Soviet imports the German share rose from 25% in 1921 to 32.7% in 1922, Great Britain being driven back to second place with 18.8%. This high percentage was not maintained in the expanding Soviet market of subsequent years. But 1922 was a year of German-Soviet rapprochement, in the economic sphere as well as in others; and throughout the nineteen-twenties it was Russian orders that helped to keep German heavy industry alive.

The military negotiations were wrapped in the profoundest secrecy. The German Government had to conceal measures of rearmament which were a flagrant contravention of the Versailles treaty — this was, indeed, the reason why Soviet aid was required. The Soviet Government would have found it embarrassing, both internationally and in some party circles, to admit active complicity in German rearmament. No Soviet writer or historian from that day to this has ever discussed the matter, except that, at the trial of Krestinsky and others in 1938, what was done with the full knowledge of the Politburo and on its instructions to help German rearmament was attributed to a treasonable conspiracy by Trotsky and his associates. On the German side, a few piecemeal and partial disclosures were made under the Weimar republic. Seeckt's biographer, writing in 1940 at a moment when it was permissible to speak frankly about past Soviet-German collaboration, gave many particulars of the negotiations; and there are several references in post-war German memoirs and in the records of the Krupp trial at Nuremburg. The German military and diplomatic archives now in the hands of the American and British Governments should some day supply further information. At present the story cannot be carried back with certainty before the beginning of 1921. The recently published *Documents on British Foreign Policy* reveal that a representative of Junkers, the great aircraft builders, set off for Moscow in October 1919 in a new Junkers plane, which made a landing in Lithuania; [1] but it is not known whether he eventually reached Moscow or what business he hoped to transact there. At the 1938 trial Krestinsky testified that the first approach was made by Seeckt in 1920 — presum-

---

[1] The aeroplane carried two passengers giving unidentified Turkish names. Enver was certainly one of them; since he was on the Allied list of war criminals, he had every reason to disguise his identity.

ably at the time of the Polish war — through Kopp. This testimony may well be correct, but is at present unconfirmed by other evidence. The creation of a special section in the German Ministry of War known as *Sondergruppe R* is said to date from the winter of 1920-1921. The earliest known document comes from the unpublished Trotsky archives; and it is something of a puzzle why Trotsky did not publish this and other documents from his collection at the time of the 1938 trial. The document is a report of April 7, 1921, from Kopp in Berlin to Trotsky in his capacity as president of the Military-Revolutionary Council, with copies to Lenin and Chicherin. It refers to " what we said in Moscow " (so that the matter had evidently been broached during Kopp's stay there in January and February), and describes the state of the negotiations for the establishment of three great German armament firms on Russian soil: the Albatrosswerke were to build aeroplanes, Blöhm and Voss to construct submarines, and Krupp to manfacture shells and munitions in general. The proposal was made to send five or six German technicians to Moscow to discuss details, and strict secrecy was enjoined. The document contains manuscript minutes by Lenin expressing approval and by Menzhinsky, deputy chief of the Cheka, asking to be kept informed in order that security arrangements might be made.

The precise course of the negotiations is still difficult to trace. In the last week in May 1921 the British Ambassador noticed the presence in Berlin of Krasin, who was having " meetings and luncheons and dinners with various German industrials." During the summer of 1921 an exploratory German military mission went to Moscow headed by Colonel Oskar von Niedermayer. Niedermayer, who liked to be known as the " German Lawrence " was engaged during the war on a secret mission in Persia and Afghanistan, stirring up trouble for the British on the frontiers of India; he was now a colonel in the Reichswehr, and later became professor of military geography in the University of Berlin and collaborated in a work on the geography of Soviet Russia which carried a preface by Haushofer, the famous leader of the school of geopolitics. Other members of the mission were Colonel Schubert, formerly German military attaché in Russia, and Major Tschunke, who had reported to Seeckt from Kovno in 1919. First results were inconclusive. On September 10 at a meeting of the Politburo, notes of which are in the Trotsky archives, an unidentified agent, apparently a German, reported " hesitations in German business circles " and fears lest the bargain, if it should leak out, might prejudice the impending Allied decision on Upper Silesia. The conclusion was to " play the Polish card," i. e. to harp on fears of Poland. Lenin observed that the " idea of combining military and economic negotiations is correct "; the establishment of German arms factories in Russia was to be camouflaged under the heading of " concessions." A curious detail which emerges from the record is that Krasin was at this time purchasing munitions for Soviet Russia in the United States. In the same month, Seeckt's biographer records the opening of the negotiations in Berlin. They took place for the most part in private apartments, generally in that of Major von Schleicher. The principal Soviet negotiator at this stage was Krasin. The principal German negotiators were General von Hasse, who had suc-

ceeded Seeckt as head of the Truppenamt when Seeckt
became commander-in-chief of the Reichswehr, General
von Thomsen, an aeronautical expert, and Niedermayer;
Seeckt in accordance with his habit remained in the background. In the latter part of 1921 Hasse himself visited
Moscow at the head of a mission which included an
admiral, and is reported to have had discussions with
Lebedev, the Soviet chief of staff, on action " in the event
of a Polish war."

It was characteristic of the relations between the Reichswehr and the German Government that the latter had
been kept in complete ignorance of these delicate negotiations; but Seeckt now decided to inform the Chancellor
Wirth, who was also Minister of Finance, of what was on
foot. It might be necessary to have the support of the
civil authorities, and more finance might be required than
could conveniently be furnished out of secret military
funds. Wirth turned out to be a strong supporter of the
Russian alliance, and in a letter written to Krupp nearly
twenty years later boasted of the part he had played in
secret German rearmament. It was about this time that a
bogus company known as GEFU (*Gesellschaft zur Förder-
ung Gewerblicher Unternehmungen* or Company to Promote Industrial Enterprises) was founded as a cover for
German firms engaged in these transactions. Its capital
was supplied by the government, and was fixed after the
end of the inflation at 75,000,000 Reichsmarks.

The crucial point of the discussions evidently came early
in 1922. On February 7, 1922, the diary of Seeckt's adju-
tant, Von Selchow, records a secret visit of " high Russian
officers " to the Truppenamt. On February 12, according

to Hasse's diary, Radek at his insistent request had a personal meeting with Seeckt — apparently the first.[2] He asked for German help in rebuilding Russia's armament industries and in the training of Soviet officers, and complained of the closeness of German relations with the west, especially with Great Britain — to which Seeckt replied that Germany needed to flirt with Britain as a counterweight to France. The Soviet negotiators in these talks are said to have held out the hope that Soviet Russia, if equipped with German aid, would make war on Poland in the spring. But, if so, this can hardly have represented a serious intention of the Soviet Government; the negotiators were merely applying Lenin's injunction to "play the Polish card." A letter from Seeckt to Hasse of May 1922 shows clearly that no agreement on military action had been reached, though Seeckt ardently desired such an agreement and hoped that "the enemy" would believe that it already existed. The first German officers and engineers appear to have gone to Soviet Russia early in 1922; and, after the signature of the Rapallo treaty in April, events moved still more quickly. Krestinsky, the Soviet Ambassador, negotiated directly with Hasse; in July a Soviet agent named Rosenblatt — perhaps the same who had reported to the Politburo in Moscow in the previous September — was received by Seeckt; and on July 29, 1922, what was described as a " preliminary commercial agreement " was signed in great secrecy. Its text has apparently not yet come to light. In September 1922, Krasin who was passing through Smolensk, wrote to his

[2] Seeckt's biographer records a first meeting in the autumn of 1921; but this looks like a confusion of dates.

wife: "I am writing this in a small house near the aerodrome which is full of German aviators." Junkers had a factory near Moscow. Shells, and presumably also guns, were manufactured by Krupp in several Russian factories and exported to Germany. A tank factory was established near Kazan with training facilities for German officers. On the other hand the project for building submarines in Russia seems to have broken down. Nothing further is heard of this; and in 1922 a Dutch company sponsored and financed by the German Ministry of Marine was established at the Hague, and placed orders in Holland, Sweden, Finland and Spain for submarines which were constructed under the supervision of German naval officers and tested by German crews. Some of these seem to have been built for the Soviet navy. A Russian chemist has described the prolonged efforts to establish a poison-gas factory 30 miles from Samara, using premises which had been designed for that purpose during the war but never completed. But these efforts also ended in failure, partly owing to Russian incompetence, partly owing to the inadequacies of the processes employed by the German firm, Hugo Stolzenberg of Hamburg.

The beginning of the political negotiations lagged behind that of the economic and military negotiations. Once the Soviet Government had adopted the policy of seeking normal relations with capitalist countries, it had everything to gain from a political agreement with Germany which would end or mitigate its isolated position among the European Powers. German diplomacy, on the other hand, far more than the German army or German industry, still leaned towards the west, and feared the probable repercussions on the attitude of the western Powers of any German entanglement in the east. Berendt, at this time head of the eastern department of the German Foreign Office, was known as a bitter anti-Bolshevik; and Wiedenfeld in Moscow is said to have been hostile to any further development of relations with the Soviet Government. These inhibitions were removed or weakened by the League of Nations decision on the division of Upper Silesia issued on October 12, 1921, which was universally resented in Germany and caused a strong revulsion of feeling against the west. Immediately after this decision Baron Ago von Maltzan, who was connected by marriage with heavy industry and was known as a strong "easterner," was appointed head of the eastern department of the Foreign Office. *The Times* of October 13, 1921, reported from Berlin that the German-Soviet commercial negotiations were "intended to pave the way to a political understanding." D'Abernon was told many years later by Maltzan that a treaty had been "practically agreed to with the Russians as regards wording as early as Christmas [1921]." This was certainly untrue, but negotiations may have been begun at this time. It is certain that Radek was in Berlin in January 1922, and Radek, Rakovsky and Krasin in February; in the latter month Radek was reported as having an interview with Rathenau, who on January 31, 1922, had once more joined Wirth's government — this time as Minister for Foreign Affairs. The split in the German Foreign Office between easterners and westerners, with Rathenau himself a strong westerner, seems to have been particularly acute at this time; and few members of the Foreign Office knew exactly what was on foot. The rest of the story is clear and has often been told. The Soviet delegation to the Genoa conference, consisting of Chicherin, Litvinov, Joffe, Rakovsky and Radek, stopped in Berlin on their way to Genoa and pressed for the conclusion of an immediate Soviet-German treaty. Negotiations took place in the German Foreign Office, and a draft text was agreed on all but two points of detail. Rathenau, however, still clinging to his hope of an agreement with the Allies, and perceiving, perhaps more clearly than the Russians, that the signature of a German-Soviet treaty would wreck the conference, still held back; and both delegations proceeded to Genoa with the treaty unsigned, with the draft incomplete and with its very existence unsuspected outside the inner circle of the German Foreign Office and the Soviet delegation.

When the conference opened, Chicherin cleverly embroiled Lloyd George and Barthou with one another on the issue of disarmament, and entered into private negotiations with the British delegation for a settlement of debts and claims. The German delegation, headed by Wirth, the Chancellor, and by Rathenau, was thoroughly alarmed by these symptoms of Anglo-Soviet amity; and Maltzan frightened his colleagues still further by assuring them that one of the baits offered to the Soviet Government was a revival of Russian reparations claims against Germany which had explicitly been kept open in the Versailles treaty. The assertion was untrue, but had its effect. The German delegation was in a depressed state of mind when at 1 a. m. on the morning of Easter Sunday, April 16, 1922, Joffe telephoned to them to propose a meeting later in the day at the neighbouring resort of Rapallo to

complete the unfinished treaty. Rathenau's biographer has
described how the principal members of the delegation
assembled in their pyjamas in Rathenau's bedroom, and
debated the question to go or not to go to Rapallo. Hasse,
Seeckt's representative in the secret military negotiations,
was present at Genoa in the German delegation, but is
not known to have participated in this famous bedroom
scene. The reluctance of Rathenau was now finally over-
borne by Wirth and Maltzan. Next morning, after two
perfunctory attempts to telephone to Lloyd George's adviser on Russian questions, E. F. Wise, who on the first
occasion was still in bed and on the second had left for
a picnic, the Soviet invitation was accepted. The day was
spent in filling up the gaps in the draft, and at 5 o'clock
the Treaty of Rapallo was signed.

The fact of signature was more important than the
formal contents of the treaty. It provided for a resumption
of full diplomatic and consular relations. Germany waived
all claims against Soviet Russia on account of nationalized
German enterprises " on the condition that the government of the RSFSR does not meet analogous claims of
other states." The economic clauses were so drafted as to
preclude participation of Germany in any international
consortium formed to deal jointly with Russia: this was
the main purpose of the agreement on the Soviet side.
The conclusion of the treaty disrupted the tottering frame-
work of the Genoa conference. After vain attempts to
save something from the wreck, it broke up without
registering any result. The anger with which the Rapallo
treaty was received by the Allies was a key to its importance. Hitherto the Allies had been able to deal with

Germany and Soviet Russia separately; the ideological barrier had prevented them from making common cause in self defence. Now the two outcasts from the Versailles system had joined hands. The effect on the diplomatic map of Europe was quite incalculable. Soviet Russia had regained a foothold in the capitalist world with pretensions to resume the rank and status of a great Power. " The policy of strangling Germany," said Radek at the fourth congress of Comintern in November 1922, implied in fact the destruction of Russia as a great Power; for, no matter how Russia is governed, it is always to her interest that Germany should exist. . . . A Russia weakened to the utmost by the war could neither have remained a great Power nor acquired the economic and technical means for her industrial reconstruction, unless she had in the existence of Germany a counter-weight to the preponderance of the Allies." It was a striking change when Soviet spokesmen began to invoke the eternal interests of Russia and to use the traditional arguments of diplomacy.

The German Government was less confident in what it had done. A rumour went the rounds, and was widely believed, that Rathenau, frightened by the indignation of the western Powers, had proposed to the Soviet delegation to cancel the treaty. The westerners in the Foreign Office were shocked and, in their relations with the western Powers, defensively apologetic. The Rapallo Treaty was represented to the British Ambassador as a sudden and unpremeditated act; nothing, he was told, with an accuracy so precise as to border on falsehood, had been " initialled " in Berlin before the departure of the delegation for Genoa. A few days later he was " formally and deliberately assured that the subject of military preparations had never been mentioned between the Germans and the Russians "—which may have been true of the Rapallo negotiators, though Seeckt's biographer records that Chicherin " appealed to the Chancellor quite openly for the presence of German officers in Russia." A month later Wirth informed the Reichstag with equal emphasis that " the Rapallo treaty contains no secret political or military agreement." This two-faced attitude was symptomatic of exactly what Germany had gained from Rapallo. The treaty established a balance. The German Government could manoeuvre freely between east and west, playing off the two rivals against one another, disclaiming any firm or irrevocable commitment to either, extorting concessions from the one by threatening to fall into the arms of the other, and always keeping its own choice open. This was the policy which was to serve Germany in good stead for the next seven years.

CHAPTER IV

GERMANY FACES BOTH WAYS

THE RAPALLO TREATY was a turning point in the foreign policies both of Germany and of Soviet Russia, and the most conspicuous landmark in European diplomacy between Versailles and Locarno. It enhanced the status and prestige of both parties, and staked out the claim of both to be restored to the select company of great Powers. Full diplomatic relations between the two countries were restored for the first time since 1918. Krestinsky became Soviet Ambassador in Berlin, presenthis credentials to Ebert on August 2, 1922. Brockdorff-Rantzau, who went Moscow as German Ambassador three months later, was a striking personality. A career diplomat of unusual flexibility and unusually wide interests, he is said to have won the praise of Kaiser William II as " the only sensible man among my diplomats — he has understood how to deal even with Social-Democrats." To this skill and foresight he owed his appointment as Minister of Foreign Affairs by Ebert in February 1919. At Versailles he made a dramatic and violent protest against the peace terms presented to the German delegation, returned to Berlin and resigned office. He remained a strong anti-Bolshevik and condemned the policy of *rapprochement* with Soviet Russia — so much so that, when after more than three years' retirement he was suggested as ambassador to Moscow, Seeckt raised strong objections. These fears proved groundless. Brockdorff-Rantzau quickly came to the conclusion that, in the words of his biographer, "the evil of Versailles can be corrected from Moscow." He treated the German Foreign Office with the contempt of one who once had been its head, and mistrusted Stresemann, but kept in close touch with Krupp, Stinnes, Felix Deutsch and other great industrialists. Chicherin is said to have greeted him with satisfaction as "the man of Versailles"; and the personal friendship which sprang up between the two men, based on common tastes in music and on common hostility to the west, helped to smooth the path of German-Soviet friendship in the next five years.

While the Soviet Government had shown itself more eager than the German Government to conclude the treaty, its acceptance, once the initial fear had been overcome, was more whole-hearted in Germany than in Russia. The treaty was generally hailed as the first independent stroke of German policy since Versailles. It put Germany back into the position which geography had assigned to her of being able to manoeuvre on both her flanks, alternately seeking the support of the west against the east and of the east against the west; it was the confirmation of a traditional German policy. Only the confirmed "westerners" of the Social-Democratic Party looked on it with mistrust, and they did not carry their opposition to the point of a vote. Generals of the old order like Ludendorff and Hoffmann, or the eccentric industrialist turned sculptor and patron of the arts, Arnold Rechberg, or Hitler, just beginning to be known as the leader of a tiny group of " national socialists," might still harp on the crusade against Bolshevism. But these were now little more than the lunatic fringe of German foreign policy. Differences remained about the respective weight to be attached to the eastern and western aspects of that policy. But that Germany must face both east and west, that Rapallo, as the symbol of German-Soviet friendship, was one essential ingredient of German policy, was henceforth accepted by all parties, from extreme nationalists to Communists inclusive.

On the Soviet side the divisions went deeper, and the Rapallo treaty became involved in the confusions of policy which attended the illness and death of Lenin. For Soviet Russia, it seemed to represent a new departure — the tacit relinquishment of the hope of world revolution in favour of an alliance with one sector of a divided capitalist world; the political implications of this change of front were realized only gradually, and acted on with many hesitations and fluctuations. It was unreservedly accepted by Narkomindel, the People's Commissariat of Foreign Affairs; Chicherin became the firmest and most convinced supporter of German-Soviet friendship. But the two years after Rapallo were years of keen and incessant rivalry between Narkomindel and Comintern. Radek, who in these years spent more time in Berlin than in Moscow and was still Comintern's principal agent in Germany, worked untiringly to continue and strengthen the Rapallo policy of which he had been the first begetter, so that the rivalry between Zinoviev and Chicherin was complicated and intensified by dissension between Zinoviev and Radek — a dissension which turned specifically on the relation of the

Rapallo policy to the cause of international revolution. When Lenin was finally stricken down at the end of 1922, the only force capable of reconciling these discords was removed. In 1922 and 1923 the influence of Zinoviev and Comintern, though no longer standing where it did in the first three years of the revolution, was still far from negligible. The policy of " socialism in one country " was not heard of before 1924.

The events of 1923 dramatically illustrated what Rapallo did, and did not, mean. The year opened with the French occupation of the Ruhr. Two months earlier the Wirth coalition government had been overthrown and succeeded by a " business men's " government under Cuno, a director of the Hamburg-Amerika Line. Cuno and Seeckt were personal friends, and the new regime represented the alliance between industry and the Reichswehr in its most naked form. Intimidated by the French display of force in the Ruhr, the German Government declared a policy of passive resistance. Any direct appeal to German-Soviet solidarity would have been a red rag to the French, and was not attempted. When, however, Foch paid a ceremonial visit to Warsaw in May 1923 with the obvious aim of cementing the Franco-Polish alliance against Germany, the Soviet Government intimated that if Poland attacked Germany the Red Army would move against Poland: this may well be called the first political dividend accruing to Germany from the Rapallo treaty. Radek went much further in trying to draw the logical consequences from Rapallo. The German Communist Party had no line of its own on the French occupation. It refused to debate the question at the party congress at Leipzig which was in session when the invasion occurred, and was content to combine denunciation of the French action with denunciation of the German Government: " Beat Poincaré on the Ruhr and Cuno on the Spree " was the headline of the *Rote Fahne* on January 23, 1923. But Radek perceived the difficulty of reconciling Rapallo with a purely negative attitude on the part of the German party and of Comintern. True to the ideas first adumbrated by some of his visitors in the Moabit prison in 1919, he now sought to bring about an alliance between the German Communists and the German nationalists of the extreme Right (the elements to which the label " Fascists " was just beginning to be applied) in support of a policy of active opposition to France. A young nationalist adventurer named Schlageter, a former member of the Freikorps, was executed by the French early in 1923 for attempted sabotage in the occupied territory, and became a hero of the German nationalists. The new policy came to be known as the " Schlageter line." In Germany Communists appeared on the same platforms with nationalists to denounce France and the western Powers. At the session of the executive committee of Comintern in Moscow in June 1923 Radek delivered an emotional eulogy of this young adventurer and pleaded for an alliance with the German nationalists engaged in the fight against Allied imperialism. The great majority of the national-minded masses belonged, he now declared, not to the camp of the capitalists, but to the camp of the workers. The speech was reprinted in *Rote Fahne*, and produced sympathetic articles from Moeller van den Bruck, the intellectual of the Nazi movement, and Reventlow, a well-known journal-

ist of the extreme Right. Fröhlich, a member of the
central committee of the German Communist Party, wrote
in the same vein in the *Rote Fahne*; and the four contri-
butions were reprinted in a pamphlet which ran through
several editions. The Rapallo policy was giving the German Communists some queer bed-fellows.

The " Schlageter line " did not win universal acceptance among the rank and file of the German party. Under
the leadership of Brandler, who belonged to the Right
wing of the party and believed in a " united front " with
the Social-Democrats rather than with the nationalists,
the party central committee called for public demonstrations against the Fascists — a so-called " anti-Fascist day "
— on Sunday, July 29. The police replied by prohibiting
street meetings, and the question then arose whether this
prohibition should be defied at the risk of a serious clash
with the police. At this point the divided party sought
advice from Moscow. The leaders of Comintern were
dispersed on holiday. Zinoviev and Bukharin replied with
a telegram encouraging the German party to go ahead.
Radek, anxious for the fate of the " Schlageter line " and of
the Rapallo policy, telegraphed back that Comintern was
" driving the party to a July defeat." Hastening to
Moscow, he induced the praesidium of the executive committee of Comintern on July 26, in Zinoviev's absence, to
advise the abandonment of the demonstrations. According
to an account given six months later by Zinoviev, Trotsky
was consulted in his absence and refused to give an
opinion; but " some of our comrades " supported Radek.
The reference here is to Stalin, who thus makes his first
appearance on the stage of German-Soviet relations. A

letter from him to Zinoviev of this period has been preserved — unfortunately its exact date is uncertain — concluding with the cautious verdict that " the Germans must be curbed and not spurred on."

It was not long before the controversy about the " anti-Fascist day " looked like a storm in a teacup. By the beginning of August 1923 an internal crisis was evidently approaching in Germany. Passive resistance in the Ruhr was breaking down. Inflation had reached hitherto un-imagined heights. A strike of bank-note printers hit the tottering regime in its most sensitive spot, and developed into a general strike in Berlin. On August 11 the now completely discredited Cuno government resigned. The German Communist Party was, as usual, divided in its attitude to the strike which, in the absence of effective cooperation between the parties of the Left, gradually fizzled out. The situation remained none the less extremely tense; and revolution in Germany seemed imminent for the first time since March 1920. Stresemann was invited to form a cabinet on the basis of what was called the " great coalition " including all the bourgeois parties, ex-cept the extreme Right, and the Social-Democrats; his programme was to end passive resistance and seek agree-ment with the Allies, particularly with Great Britain. These events affected the leaders in Moscow in two ways. In the first place, the development in Germany of what was to all appearances an acute revolutionary situation encouraged those who still actively pinned their hopes on world revolution. Secondly, the threat of a rapprochement between the new German Government and the west con-jured up once again the bogey of a coalition of the capitalist

powers against Soviet Russia and undermined the very
foundations of Rapallo. Under the impetus of these two
forces, it was decided that the time had come to stimulate
revolution in Germany; and the leaders of the German
Communist Party were summoned to Moscow. Zinoviev
was now joined by Trotsky in an optimistic estimate of
the ripeness of Germany for the long-awaited proletarian
revolution. The volatile Radek quickly changed sides and
became an advocate of revolutionary action. Stalin retired
to the seat in the background which he was still careful to
occupy when critical international issues were debated.

The German Communist leaders spent most of September and the first ten days of October 1923 in Moscow,
where plans for the revolution were duly laid. These
included the despatch from Russia of a number of experts
in revolution, with ample supplies of money and munitions.
The leaders, accompanied by Radek with the usual false
papers, then returned to Germany where, in accordance
with the prearranged strategy, Brandler and two other
Communists accepted an invitation from the Social-Democrats to join a coalition government in Saxony. The
German authorities were, however, on the alert and acted
first. On the strength of some inflammatory pronouncements by Brandler and his associates, the government of
the Reich, with some stretching of its constitutional
powers, declared the Saxon Government dissolved and sent
in the Reichswehr to carry out the decision by force. The
Communists were not ready and, after some desperate talk,
no resistance was offered. In the confusion of the moment,
summons to start the insurrection reached the party in
Hamburg. The summons was obeyed, and the rising was

crushed with much bloodshed after two days' street fighting. The great German revolution had once more ended in
a fiasco. In the German party Brandler was the obvious
scapegoat. In Moscow, in the prolonged recriminations
which followed, Trotsky stuck to the view that the objective conditions for a revolution had been present and
that " only a revolutionary party was lacking." Zinoviev,
perhaps more aptly, but rather late in the day, observed
that the German bourgeoisie was not led by Rasputins,
and that the German Social-Democrats were stronger and
more effective than the Mensheviks. He had at least the
satisfaction of bringing about the disgrace of Radek, who
was never again allowed to concern himself in German
affairs.

Paradoxically the abortive Communist rising of October
1923, which seemed a denial of the Rapallo policy, served
in the end to confirm and reinforce it. This happened for
two reasons, one German, the other Russian. In spite of
the ease and vigour with which the impending Communist
rising of October 1923 had been forestalled, the Stresemann government was in desperate straits. The attempt
to come to terms with the west after the calling off of
passive resistance still hung fire. The French troops were
still in the Ruhr, and hoped for credits from Great Britain
proved unobtainable. The " great coalition " of German
parties was fast breaking up; and Germany was a prey
to every kind of internal division. A military dictatorship
under Seeckt was seriously canvassed: Schleicher was an
ardent advocate of this solution, which was blocked only
by dissensions on the Right about the suitability of the
candidate. A fortnight after the Saxon affair the Reichs-

wehr had to intervene in far more difficult conditions in Bavaria to suppress a Hitler-Ludendorff *putsch*. Faced with these embarrassments, the Stresemann government could ill afford to add to them by embroiling itself with Soviet Russia. An official blind eye was turned on Russian support of the German Communists. Krasin, who was at the Soviet Embassy in Berlin for the anniversary celebration on November 7, 1923, noted the presence among the guests of large numbers of German industrialists and bankers. On December 1, Stresemann, now no longer Chancellor, but Minister for Foreign Affairs in another coalition cabinet, wrote to Brockdorff-Rantzau that, while the financing of the German Communists with Russian gold " makes our relations with Soviet Russia very difficult," it was none the less vital to maintain those relations intact. The policy of Rapallo stood. The effect of the abortive rising on Soviet policy was more positive. At long last the Bolshevik leaders abandoned the mirage of the German revolution. Never again were the expectations of an early revolution in Germany allowed to override the normal considerations of foreign policy. Never again would Comintern pursue an independent policy of its own. The star of Zinoviev was setting. The repeated failure of the German revolution, so damaging to the assumptions originally made by Lenin and all the Bolshevik leaders, was the most powerful single cause of the change of front inaugurated by Stalin in 1924 under the slogan of " socialism in one country." Into this new pattern of Soviet policy the Rapallo treaty fitted far more easily than into the pattern prevailing at the time of its signature. For the

next three or four years it was the undisputed cornerstone
of Soviet policy in Europe.

The first half of 1924 was a period of general détente in
international relations. It witnessed the coming into power
of the Labour Government in Great Britain under Mac-
Donald and of the Left coalition in France under Herriot;
the formal recognition of the Soviet Government by the
principal European countries; the liquidation of the Ruhr
adventure; and the drafting of the Dawes report on
German reparations. It was an uneventful period in
German-Soviet relations. The German Communist Party,
which had been banned under the state of emergency proclaimed in October, 1923, resumed its legal existence on
March 1, 1924. But while its candidates could still command a large electoral vote, its active membership had
dropped to less than half, and was now only 120,000. In
May two German Communists under arrest in Berlin
escaped into the premises of the Soviet Trade Delegation,
where they were chased and re-arrested by the German
police in violation of the diplomatic immunity which the
building enjoyed. But, though sharp words were exchanged, it was clear that neither side wished this incident
to disturb the even tenour of German-Soviet friendship.
When, however, in August 1924 delegates of the western
Powers and Germany met in conference in London and
approved the recommendations of the Dawes report for
a large loan to Germany to be raised in western Europe
and in the United States against specific pledges of German
assets, when later in the year the issue of the Dawes loan
proved a brilliant success, and when in the following year
the political consequences were drawn in the famous

Locarno treaty, then German-Soviet relations were once more subjected to fundamental debate. Germany's central and ambivalent position, facing east and facing west, became the crucial point of European diplomacy.

The reasons for Germany's dual dependence on east and west and for her resulting dual policy were complex. The initial act of the German Government after the armistice in rejecting the two trainloads of Soviet grain for the sake of the much greater benefactions which the United States could offer was symbolic of Germany's basic dependence on the west. It was true that this emergency was temporary, and that Germany would have been physically capable of feeding herself and constructing a working economy not dependent on foreign aid. But such a departure would have meant a radical re-planning of the whole economy which could only be effected as the result of a major social revolution; and the attitude of the population after 1918 showed that a majority of the workers were ready to acquiesce in the maintenance of the existing social order, even if they did not actively support it. The capitalist order in the form in which it existed in Germany, with industry and the army in the saddle, was, however, already threatened with bankruptcy before 1914. The first world war was a gambler's throw to make it once more viable by acquiring fresh regions of the world to exploit and develop. After 1918, with this hope destroyed and even Germany's pre-war territories gravely curtailed, the one possibility of restoring the German economy on its old basis was the inflow of foreign subsidies and foreign investment on a large scale. It was with some such hope in view that the Weimar republic

sent Wiedfeld, a director of Krupps, to Washington as its
first ambassador at the end of 1921. The Dawes loan, and
the successive waves of American investment in Germany
which followed it, were an heroic attempt to apply this
policy. What was not realized was that no short-term
expedient would suffice to restore the " normal " working
of the shattered German economy. The German economy
in the conditions of the 1920's could be kept going on its
former basis only through cumulative foreign investment;
and, failing either a restoration of profitable oversea
markets or a socialization of the economy which would
have stimulated domestic consumption, these investments
flowed into the unproductive channel of largely superfluous
" public works." Once this flow stopped — as it did in
1929 — the whole edifice was bound to collapse. But in
1924 and 1925 nothing of this was understood. The
miracle of a restoration of the German economy by the
grace of Wall Street seemed to have occurred. The Stresemann policy of stabilization through foreign aid, which
was the essence of the Dawes plan, had been eagerly
accepted by all German parties except those of the
extreme Right and the extreme Left. The political stabilization in the west, which was the essence of Locarno,
was a corollary of the Dawes plan.

German dependence on the west did not, however,
preclude dependence on the east. German industry, and
particularly heavy industry, which was its core and centre,
found its natural and only available outlet in the east —
the more so since its subsidiary oversea markets had been
captured by the Allies. Nor was the other major force in
the formulation of German policy, the German army,

prepared for any permanent arrangement which made Germany turn her back on the east to become a junior partner in a western alliance. The army had suffered defeat at the hands of the west, and its honour required that that defeat should be avenged. On this point all thought alike. Even those German generals and officers who would have accepted Allied help to destroy Bolshevism thought of the destruction of Bolshevism as the prelude to a reconstitution of the German-Russian alliance which would one day enable Germany to turn against the west. The cautious Seeckt, who so rigorously discouraged any kind of military adventure, in 1919 described " war against the west in alliance with the east " as " a firm necessity for me " and " my outlook for a distant future." The two strongest forces in Germany, heavy industry and the army, were both for different reasons still deeply committed to the Russian alliance. German foreign policy in its present phase could only hold a careful balance between east and west and draw the maximum advantage from both orientations. It was Stresemann's merit as a statesman that he conducted this difficult policy with supreme skill through six critical years.

The position of Soviet Russia was far simpler. The nightmare of Soviet politicians was a combination of all the capitalist countries to overthrow Soviet power; it seemed at times incredible that the capitalists should continue to be too short-sighted to form such a combination. The sole salvation for Soviet Russia lay in the divisions within the capitalist world. The incipient political discords between the United States and Japan, between Britain and the United States, between Britain and France were in turn eagerly scanned and discussed. Unfortunately none of these rifts developed far. In the middle 1920's the one effective division in the capitalist world was between the victorious Allies and defeated Germany. Hence Soviet Russia had no real freedom of manoeuvre; since the friendship of the Allies was not to be had at any price, friendship with Germany — the policy of Rapallo — was the one available alternative. The scarcely concealed purpose of the Dawes plan was to draw Germany into the orbit of the west, and especially of American capital. American diplomacy, seconding the efforts of American finance, had been tireless in its support. While the plan was under consideration in July and August 1924, the American Secretary of State Hughes had toured the principal capitals of Europe campaigning in favour of it; some months later Stresemann wrote to the American Ambassador that the German Government had accepted it " largely by your suggestion and recommendation." Thus the Dawes plan was read in Moscow as the first move in a campaign to win Germany for the west. The adoption of the plan, said the Communist spokesman in the Reichstag, would leave the great German capitalists in power side by side with the capitalists of the Entente: every one else—the workers, the employees, the middle classes—would be sacrificed. According to a later report in a French newspaper, Chicherin, while the London conference on the Dawes plan was sitting in August 1924, had a meeting in Wiesbaden, where he was taking a cure, with leaders of the German National Party, including Westarp and Tirpitz; and some sort of neutrality pact between Germany and Soviet Russia was adumbrated. Whether this was correct or not, Germany's shift towards the west at once produced a coolness in Moscow. In October 1924, Chicherin speaking in the All-Union Executive Committee in Moscow, declared that the Dawes plan had deprived Germany of her freedom of action, and Stalin denounced it in *Pravda* as meaning "the financial enslavement of Germany" by the west. Negotiations for a commercial treaty which had been in progress between Moscow and Berlin in a desultory fashion for more than a year visibly languished. The German Communist Party, which had secured 3,700,000 votes in the Reichstag election of May 1924, polled only 2,700,000 in the election of December. Not only the German Government, but the German people, seemed to be turning from east to west; and the Soviet leaders were haunted by the constant fear that Germany might break away from the Rapallo line, leaving Soviet Russia isolated and helpless. It was not recognized that German-Soviet friendship was in fact as indispensable to Germany as to Soviet Russia, and that one partner had as much, and as little, freedom of manoeuvre, as the other. The situation was not so dangerous for the Soviet Government as it seemed.

The battle for Germany was fought out in a more acute form in the following year on the issue of Locarno and the entry of Germany into the League of Nations. During the London conference on the Dawes plan in August 1924, unofficial talks took place on the possibility of Germany joining the League, and in September the German Government sought information from the principal Allied Powers about the conditions of admission. This action produced anxious enquiries from the Soviet Embassy in Berlin. By accident or design, a letter was published from Chicherin to a friend in Berlin in which Germany's design to join the League was described as likely to " come into collision with the Rapallo policy." Stresemann began the balancing game which he pursued with consummate dexterity for the next 18 months. He explained to Chicherin that the point on which Germany's discussions with the League Powers turned was precisely the question of Russia. As an unarmed country, Germany was not in a position to fulfil any military obligations under the sanctions article of the League Covenant and could not expose German territory to the danger of becoming a battle-ground. On the other hand Germany's permanent membership of the council of the League (which had been promised to her) would in effect give her a veto on all action to be taken under the sanctions article. The implication was not absent that German membership of the League would in some sense be a safeguard of Soviet interests.

These arguments failed to carry conviction; and, when by a German memorandum to the western Allies of February 9, 1925, the issue was broadened out into a proposal for a security pact with the west, the Soviet objections were confirmed and reinforced. They were unequivocally defined by Chicherin in a speech to the All-Union Congress of Soviets in May:

If the policy of the pact of guarantee with the western Powers proposed by the German Government at the instigation of England should be put into operation, if Germany should enter the League of Nations, then, despite the wish of the German Government, it will by the force of things find itself in a position which will make it scarcely possible to continue, at least in the same degree as hitherto, the relations established between us.

The Soviet Government testified its displeasure in a manner which was afterwards to become familiar by arresting two travelling German students on a charge of espionage and accusing a member of the German Embassy of having inspired their activities. Brockdorff-Rantzau tendered his resignation in protest against Germany's threatened abandonment of her ally, and was with difficulty induced by Hindenburg to withdraw it. The idea of corresponding negotiations between Germany and Russia was mooted by supporters of an eastern orientation in Berlin. Stresemann held back for a somewhat disingenuous reason. He was not against negotiations; but " I would not care," he records himself as saying, " to conclude a treaty with Russia so long as our political situation in other directions was not cleared up, as I wanted to be able to answer the question whether we had a treaty with Russia in the negative."

This attitude was hardly calculated to placate the Soviet Government. Litvinov, the deputy Commissar for Foreign Affairs, was in Berlin in June, and again in September, to protest against Germany's impending turn towards the west. Chicherin made a subtler move. In August he concluded a convention with Poland for the regulation of frontier incidents — a frequent symptom of the endemic friction between the two countries; and, at the end of September, with the Locarno meeting already announced for October 5, he paid a friendly visit to Warsaw, where he was received with much solicitude. Since anything concerning Poland always acted as a barometer in German-Russian relations, the hint was not lost. From Warsaw Chicherin moved on to Berlin. On the evening of September 30 he had a long conversation with Stresemann ranging over the whole field of German-Soviet affairs. On October 1 he was entertained to lunch by the Chancellor, Luther, General von Seeckt being one of the guests. On October 2, it was announced that the German Government had at last approved the conclusion of a commercial and consular treaty with Soviet Russia; and on the same evening, having delicately adjusted the balance in advance, Luther, Stresemann and the German delegation left for Locarno. It is said that Stresemann was still closeted with Chicherin an hour before the departure. The commercial treaty, which was accompanied by a railway convention, a navigation convention and an agreement on taxation, was signed in Moscow on October 12, 1925, four days before the initialling of the Locarno treaty and its subsidiary agreements. With the Locarno agreements was included a letter from the Allied governments to the German Government expressing the view that any obligations falling on Germany in virtue of the sanctions article of the League Covenant would always be conditioned by the geographical and other circumstances of her situation. The ratification of the Locarno treaty was opposed in the Reichstag by the same combination which had stood out against the Dawes plan — the extreme Right, which denounced it as a voluntary endorsement by Germany of the Versailles frontiers, and the Communists, who maintained that it was an attempt of " English imperialism " to " organize Europe as an English front against Soviet Russia." It was carried by 292 votes to 174.

Chicherin, having remained in Berlin while Luther and Stresemann were at Locarno, next went to Paris, where amicable discussions took place with the French Government and received wide publicity. The hint was once more not lost. In December 1925, when Stresemann's hands had been freed by the vote of the Reichstag and by the formal signature of the Locarno treaty in London, German-Soviet negotiations for a political treaty were once more taken up in Berlin. Chicherin, with a faint hint of reconciliation in his tone, declared in an interview published in the German press that Soviet Russia's fears of the consequences of Locarno did not " extend to the intentions of the German Government which are not in doubt," but only to " the objective circumstances which will be created for Germany by the Locarno treaty." Negotiations now proceeded more smoothly and were perhaps assisted by the hitch which occurred at Geneva in March 1926, when Germany's entry into the League and election to a permanent seat on the council were blocked by Brazilian and Polish claims. On April 24, 1926, a German-Soviet treaty was finally signed in Berlin. The treaty provided that, if either party were attacked " by one or more Powers," the other would " observe neutrality for the whole duration of the conflict," and that, if either party were subjected to " an economic or financial boycott " by a coalition of Powers, the other would not join in such a coalition. Litvinov at once hailed it as " an amplification of the Rapallo treaty "; and the German Chancellor, Marx, in submitting it to the Reichstag a few weeks later, stated unambiguously that it was intended to adapt the German-Russian relationship established at Rapallo to " the new political situation created by the Locarno treaties." In Germany it was compared with satisfaction to Bismarck's

famous " reinsurance treaty " with Russia in 1887, which
William II had failed to renew three years later — his
first step on the road to ruin. D'Abernon noted in his diary
that, for the first time in the history of the Weimar
republic, the vote endorsing a treaty in the Foreign Affairs
Committee of the Reichstag had been unanimous; and the
only hostile votes in the Reichstag itself came from three
dissident Communists, who reproached the German Communist Party rather late in the day with seeking to create
" a community of action between the proletariat and the
bourgeoisie on an international scale."

The Berlin treaty of April 24, 1926, was Stresemann's
answer to his own question " whether and how far a loyal
German League policy was compatible with a friendly
adjustment of Russo-German relations," and represented
in his words " the idea of combining this Locarno policy
with a consolidation of our relations with Russia." Re-
viving Bismarck's policy after a lapse of 40 years, Stresemann had shown that it was possible, as well as necessary,
to face both east and west. The reality behind Locarno
was Germany's financial dependence on the west, and
especially on the United States; the reality behind the
Berlin treaty was Germany's military dependence on
Soviet Russia, expressed in the secret agreements for the
manufacture of munitions for Germany, and the training
of German officers in prohibited weapons, on Russian soil.
It was convenient for Stresemann to appear during his
tenure of office primarily as the sponsor and protagonist
of the western face of German foreign policy. The three-
volume edition of selections from his papers which appeared after his death in German, and soon afterwards in

an English translation, referred mainly to this side of his work. But it would be chimerical to suppose that Stresemann, whose party represented first and foremost the great German industrialists and business men, was not keenly interested in the secret arrangements under which German industry operated in Soviet Russia, or was ignorant of any part of them. If and when the remaining Stresemann papers from which the selection was made are eventually published (they are now in British and American hands), they will no doubt throw further light on the Russian aspects of his policy.

The legend of Stresemann as the man of Locarno, the man who set German policy on the path of fulfilment of the Versailles treaty and of a western orientation, was originally built up in the west, and was a necessary part of the propaganda in favour of the German loans issued to American and British investors. The legend was accepted by the Nazis and by other enemies of the Locarno policy in Germany, where Stresemann's memory was subjected after 1933 to every kind of vituperation and contempt. During the second world war the wheel turned, and Stresemann was bitterly assailed both from the Soviet and from the western side by writers who depicted him as a monster of duplicity, an extreme German nationalist and a precursor of the Nazis themselves. Both pictures are wide of the mark. Stresemann was a German patriot who valued the western connexion, the League of Nations and Locarno not for any sentimental or ideological reason, but for the advantages which they brought to his country; for the same reason he valued the eastern connexion, however little he, in common with most German industrialists, appreciated the theory or practice of the Bolsheviks. He exercised a great economy of truth when he repeatedly assured the Allies that Germany was loyally carrying out her obligations under the disarmament clauses of the Versailles treaty. But it is customary for foreign ministers to deny all knowledge of the secret operations of other departments — or even of their own; and it would be unfair to attribute these official deceptions to any personal idiosyncracy in Stresemann's character. Few statesmen fail in an emergency to recognize a duty to lie for their country.

Stresemann's policy, like that of all German politicians, civilian or military, of that period was marked by the " craftiness " of a weak and unarmed country set between two far more powerful neighbours, standing in need of both, and compelled to manoeuvre between them. As Stresemann wrote at the time, the choice between east and west was not open: such a choice could only be made when backed by military force. The drama of German-Soviet relations in the Locarno period was that, while Germany played off Soviet Russia and the western Allies against one another, Soviet Russia was trying — far less successfully — to play off the western Allies against Germany. The time would come in the nineteen-thirties when Germany could afford to abandon the policy of the balance and make a choice between east and west; and by that time Soviet Russia was also strong enough to make a choice between Germany and the western Allies. But in the nineteen-twenties neither of these conditions was realized. Soviet Russia was bound to Germany by her inability to come to terms with the west. Germany could not dispense with any of the advantages which she received whether from the west or from the east. It is true that Stresemann's achievement lacked any lasting quality. In common with the industrialists and financiers of all countries, including his own, he failed to realize that the foundations of Germany's pre-war economy had been destroyed beyond repair; and he hoped against hope that the structure could be rebuilt on the shifting sands of loans and credits from the west. His service to his country was, however, real: he carried out with superb mastery the policy, essential to the Germany of his day, of facing both ways.

Chapter V

THE END OF WEIMAR

THE YEAR 1926 was the high-water mark of German-Soviet relations. The conclusion of the treaty of April 1926 was followed by the granting to Soviet Russia by the German banks of credits to the total amount of 300,000,000 marks; in June, " thanks to the cooperation of the German Government," interest on these credits was fixed at 9.4% per annum. In October 1926 a distinguished group of Reichstag deputies visited Moscow. Early in December, when Chicherin again visited Berlin, he remarked to the press on the improvement in German-Soviet relations since his previous visit a year earlier. From this point, however, a slow decline set in which, though its even tenour was interrupted by frequent ups and downs, continued more or less regularly till Hitler brought friendly relations to a full stop some months after his accession to power. The decline in German-Soviet amity had several causes, both general and particular. Both parties after 1926 were beginning to be conscious of their strength and stature in the world. They were no longer the scorned and bewildered outcasts who tremblingly came together at Rapallo; both could now feel that other connexions and other friendships were open to them. On the Soviet side the suspicions roused by the Dawes and Locarno policies had perhaps never been entirely allayed. A certain desire was felt to show that, if Germany could play off the west against the east, Soviet Russia could also play off the west against Germany. On the German side, the cooling off process was assisted by a number of minor episodes which made it increasingly difficult for Stresemann to succeed in his balancing feat between east and west.

The first of these incidents was the dismissal of Seeckt. The excuses for it were trivial; the cause was apparently personal rather than political. Seeckt had never been forgiven for his hostility to the old generals — the Ludendorffs, the Von der Goltzes and the Lüttwitzes; in Junker circles he was still " Seeckt the traitor " and " red Seeckt." Hindenburg, who had been elected President of the Reich in 1925, was easily influenced by these circles, and had vanities of his own. He still liked to think of himself as the first soldier of Germany, and resented the military authority exercised by Seeckt and the military prestige enjoyed by him. Nor was Seeckt popular with his own staff; Schleicher is said to have been one of those who intrigued against him. It is significant of the power and independence of the Reichswehr as a state within a state that the government was apparently not consulted on so important a decision. According to a statement issued by Stresemann, " General von Seeckt's departure was solely a matter of military discipline, and was decided exclusively between the Reichswehr Minister and President von Hindenburg without any action on the part of the cabinet." The occurrence had no direct bearing on German-Soviet relations and betokened no change of policy. Nevertheless Seeckt had held all the threads of German-Soviet secret military collaboration in his hands and was particularly associated with it. It is related by Seeckt's biographer that, when Brockdorff-Rantzau, the German Ambassador to Moscow, died in 1928, the Russians asked for Seeckt as his successor; if so, the request was not granted.

A much more important incident occurred in December 1926. In the autumn three ships loaded with munitions for the Reichswehr arrived in Stettin from Leningrad. It was certainly not the first such shipment and can hardly have been the first that became known to the German Social-Democratic Party. But on this occasion the party decided to use the information as a card in the political game to discredit the Reichswehr. That some scruples were felt is suggested by the fact that it was disclosed in the first instance not to any German organ, but to the Berlin correspondent of the English Liberal newspaper, the *Manchester Guardian*, which published an article on December 2, 1926, revealing that aircraft, gas and bombs were being manufactured in Soviet Russia for the Reichswehr. Next day the information was reproduced from this source in the Social-Democratic newspaper, *Vorwärts*. In the Reichstag, on December 16, 1926, Scheidemann, a former Social-Democratic Chancellor, launched a major attack on the Reichswehr, describing it as "an armed power which in its essential parts conducts its own policy which is directly opposed to the policy of democracy and of peace." In a speech interrupted by loud and frequent protests, he explained the functions of *Sondergruppe R* in the Reichswehr Ministry, which ever since 1923 had had 70,000,000 marks a year at its disposal, and of GEFU which, for better concealment, had recently been replaced by a similar organization called WIKO (*Wirtschafts-kontor*). He disclosed with a certain vagueness of detail, but with substantial accuracy, the whole process of sending Reichswehr officers to Russia with false passports for training and of importing from Russia war material manufactured there by German firms.

The most astonishing thing about these revelations was the negligible effect which they produced. Chicherin in an interview in the *Berliner Tageblatt* would offer only one comment on them: " Made in England." *Pravda* was stung into a bland statement that " certain German firms several years ago created three factories for the production of material necessary for our defence," including " aeroplanes, gases, shells etc.," and *Izvestiya* in an article signed by Radek explained that " the USSR does not refuse the services of foreign technicians in order to strengthen its defences against foreign imperialists." The establishment of war industries by German firms in Russia was thus admitted, but not the export of war material to Germany or the training of German personnel. Thereafter the Soviet press relapsed into the complete silence on the subject which it has always maintained before and since. In Germany, the Communists and the parties of the Right combined to denounce the treachery of the Social-Democrats in making these allegations, while leaving discreetly obscure the question how far the allegations were true. The notorious bitterness and recklessness of party polemics in Germany made it difficult to win credence for an attack which was for once an understatement rather than an exaggeration of real facts. But the main significance of the passive German reaction to Scheidemann's revelations was the proof it afforded of the ineffectiveness of parliamentary democracy under the Weimar republic. The real rulers of Germany were still the Reichswehr and the industrialists. The Reichstag exercised its functions within the limits of major policy determined by them. Any attempt by the political parties to exceed these limits and to interfere in vital issues such as that of Soviet-German military collaboration was not so much repelled as ignored. Scheidemann launched his anathema against the policy of the Reichswehr. The echoes died away. Nothing happened. No investigation of the charges was held, no official reply made. Seeckt's biographer states that the incident led to a " damping down " of Soviet-German cooperation. But this seems to reflect Seeckt's own bitterness at his dismissal, and is hardly borne out by other sources.

What is at first sight more surprising still is that the revelations caused no serious reaction in Allied countries. They came at a moment when, as one of the refreshing fruits of Locarno, the decision had just been taken to withdraw the Allied Military Control set up in Germany under the Versailles treaty. They might have thrown some doubt on the wisdom of that decision. But this time the Locarno policy — the determination to restore German independence and to rebuild the German economy with financial aid from the west — was so firmly rooted and so unquestioningly accepted that no arguments were likely to shake it. The Scheidemann revelations were brushed aside as something that was either too trivial to be noticed or belonged exclusively to the forgotten past. On January 31, 1927, the Allied Military Control in Germany was wound up and the remaining officers withdrawn. The formal limitations of the Versailles treaty remained, but the means of enforcing them were abandoned. Germany's military independence was in fact restored. It was this event, rather than Scheidemann's speech, which may have led to a certain "damping down" in German-Soviet relations. Though the British House of Commons was told in June 1927 that imports of arms from Russia into Germany had ceased, evidence shows that the manufacture of arms in Russia, and the sending of German personnel to Russia for training, continued down to the end of the Weimar republic and even later. But it is at any rate probable that no further expansion occurred after the beginning of 1927. Germany was now in a position to carry out measures of secret rearmament at home; and it was only where conspicuous large-scale operations were required — as perhaps for training in aviation and tank warfare — that the great open spaces of Russia presented a serious advantage. One uncovenanted result of the Allied decision to abandon military control was to make Germany less dependent on Russia and to this extent strengthen the hand of German foreign policy.

On the Soviet side 1927 was a mixed year. It was the year when the British Government raided the premises of Arcos, the Soviet trading company in London, and broke off relations with the Soviet Government. But this British step found no imitators and few sympathizers; a curious conversation at Geneva is recorded by Stresemann in which Austen Chamberlain was put very much on the defensive by Stresemann and Briand, and disowned any intention " to involve any other country in these affairs " or to undertake " a crusade against Russia." It was a year of disaster for Soviet policy in China. But this, though important in the internal struggle within the Russian Communist Party which was just coming to a head, had no influence on the course of European affairs. First and foremost, 1927 was the year of the first appearance of Soviet Russia on the Geneva stage. Now that Germany was in the League of Nations, the Soviet Government could not easily afford to be the only absentee European Power at Geneva. Now that Zinoviev was discredited and defeated, and Comintern possessed no stronger champion in the party counsels than the mild and cultivated Bukharin, the policy of compromises and peaceful cohabitation with the capitalist world was unchallenged, and could be given wider scope. Another personal element in the change of front was the gradual extrusion of Chicherin from the leading role at Narkomindel by his ambitious Deputy Commissar, Maxim Litvinov. Chicherin was a sick man as well as a personal enemy of Stalin. After 1927 his public appearances were increasingly rare, though he continued to hold the titular post till 1930. In 1927 the Soviet Government accepted invitations to be represented at the world economic conference and the preparatory commission for the disarmament conference, both held at Geneva under the auspices of the League. This was in no sense an anti-German move. But, by bringing Soviet representatives into more or less constant touch with the western Powers, it helped to bring to an end the isolation which had been an important factor in driving the Soviet Government into the arms of Germany and keeping it there. Chicherin, a strong exponent of the German orientation in Soviet policy, is believed to have opposed the *rapproche-*

ment with Geneva. Under Litvinov, Soviet diplomacy acquired new contracts and a new freedom of manoeuvre. From 1927 to 1934, when Soviet Russia finally joined the League of Nations after Hitler's accession to power, the Soviet Government was being driven slowly, and often protestingly, but none the less surely, into closer ties with the western Powers.

While Comintern seemed under the Stalinist dispensation plainly condemned to a secondary role, a step was taken by it at this time which had serious and unforeseen consequences. Since 1921 Communist parties abroad had been acting under the slogan of the " united front " which, though variously interpreted, indicated a readiness, at any rate in theory, for some sort of cooperation with other parties of the Left. It was under this ruling that the Chinese Communists had collaborated with Kuo-min-tang; and this policy, which had enjoyed Stalin's blessing, ended in a resounding disaster when Chiang Kai-shek turned on his partners. The British Communist Party had made continuous overtures to the Labour Party, where they had always been ill received, and more successful approaches to the trade unions, where Communist influence, though not predominant, was substantial. But the general strike of 1926 and the subsequent growth of hostility to Soviet Russia in the British trade unions ended all hope of friendly relations. Thus proposals were made simultaneously to modify the policy of the united front both in China and in Great Britain; and, on the supposition still universally accepted that the tactics of Comintern were general and not particular, so that what was right for one party was automatically right for all, this meant a general change of line in Comintern. Stalin at a speech at the fifteenth congress of the Russian Communist Party in December 1927 announced the approaching end of the " temporary stabilization " achieved by the capitalist world over the past four or five years — for once, not a bad guess; and the moral he drew was the need to " intensify the international struggle against reformism." Instructions were issued to China and Great Britain accordingly by the executive committee of Comintern; and the new policy was put into shape by the sixth world congress of Comintern in the summer of 1928. The manifesto issued by the congress, ranging the Social-Democrats with the Fascists, denounced them as being " on the side of the exploiters, on the side of the imperialists, on the side of the imperialist robber states and their agents," and called on the workers everywhere to fight " against reformism and Fascism for the proletarian revolution."

These proceedings had no specific refe.ence to German affairs. It was probably a coincidence that in May 1928, three months before the resolution of Comintern was passed, the German Social-Democratic Party participated for the first time for four-and-a-half years in the formation of a German Government with a Social-Democrat as Chancellor. Relations between the German Communists and the German Social-Democrats had never been anything but bitter even in the days when the Communists had been theoretically advocates of a united front. But after 1928 a new note of animosity was introduced into the dispute from the Communist side, and no occasion was missed of denouncing the Social-Democrats as " Social-Fascists " and the worst enemies of the working class. It was in the poisoned atmosphere encouraged, though not engendered, by the 1928 manifesto of Comintern that Hitler achieved his spectacular rise to power without once uniting the two major parties of the German Left against him.

The next two or three years added little that was noteworthy to the story of German-Soviet relations. The signposts were few, and not all of them pointed in the same direction. In October, 1928, the first Soviet Five-Year Plan was inaugurated. A logical conclusion from the doctrine of " socialism in one country," it portended a more exclusive concentration of Soviet policy on the domestic scene: relations with foreign countries would tend to move in accordance with the requirements of the plan. A few months before the plan was introduced the first of several mass trials on charges of industrial sabotage occurred. The accused were engineers employed in the Donetz coal mines, and among them were five Germans. It was the first time that foreigners had been involved in an important state trial in the Soviet Union, and a great outcry was raised in Germany. In the end two of the five were released before the trial, two were acquitted, and one who confessed was sentenced to a year's imprisonment but at once released in exchange for a Russian Communist detained in Germany. In December 1928 Litvinov angrily accused Germany of violating the Rapallo treaty by allowing German banks to be represented on a committee of creditors of Russia. On the other hand, a fresh economic agreement was signed at the end of 1928, and a treaty of conciliation providing machinery for the settlement of points of disagreement in January 1929. In the preparatory commission at Geneva, the Soviet delegation not only supported all German pleas for disarmament, but far outbid them, giving great satisfaction to the otherwise isolated German delegation; here the two outcasts still felt themselves outcasts, and the spirit of Rapallo was still alive. But in general the initial enthusiasm and constant preoccupation with the state of mutual relations which had marked the middle twenties were now over. What survived was a marriage of convenience, which was kept up partly out of habit and partly because its advantages to both sides were still just great enough to warrant the effort required to maintain it. Dirksen, the correct and rather colorless diplomat who succeded the explosive Brockdorff-Rantzau as German Ambassador in Moscow, typified the new spirit of German-Soviet relations.

The great economic crisis which first made itself felt in 1930 tended to strengthen the economic ties between the two countries. Germany needed the Soviet Union more than ever as a market for her shrinking exports, and the Soviet Union depended more than anything else on the products of German heavy industry to carry out the policy of industrialization. German-Soviet trade during the period of the depression declined far less steeply than world trade as a whole. But the impression remains of a slow deterioration of relations punctuated by rather frenzied attempts to pretend that all was well. In the summer of 1930 an elaborate joint statement was given out in Moscow, recording the common desire of the two governments " to surmount the difficulties that have arisen in the spirit of the Rapallo treaty and of other treaties in force between them." About the same time Litvinov

telegraphed his congratulations to the German Foreign
Minister Curtius (Stresemann had died in the previous
autumn) on the Allied evacuation of the Rhineland; and
this was perhaps the last occasion of an official Soviet pro-
nouncement on the once popular theme of Germany's
liberation from the fetters of Versailles.

The year 1931 made it clear that, whatever the state of
German-Soviet relations, the Soviet Government was looking round for other friends. In 1926 a Soviet attempt to
negotiate a debt settlement with France—still the burning
issue in Franco-Soviet relations—had been defeated by the
intervention of Poincaré, and since then relations had languished. As late as 1930 Stalin could still speak of France
as " the most aggressive and militarist of all aggressive
and militarist countries." But in March 1931 Molotov in
a speech to the All-Union Congress of Soviets went out
of his way to express eagerness to improve relations with
France. In May discussions began in Paris, and some sort
of informal understanding had apparently been reached
by the end of the year. About the same time it became
known that, after an interval of many years, friendly discussions were in progress between the Soviet and Polish
Governments for the conclusion of a non-aggression pact.
Poland was an even more sensitive spot than France in
German-Soviet relations; and Moscow did not wish to
run any risk of being off with the old love before being on
with the new. In December 1931 Stalin took the then
unusual step of granting an interview to a popular German
writer, Emil Ludwig, who happened to be visiting Moscow
and who expressed " serious fears " lest " the traditional
policy of friendship between the USSR and Germany may

be forced into the background . . . as a result of the negotiations with Poland." But Stalin's verbal reassurances were perhaps not very satisfying. His defence of the proposed Polish pact was to compare it with the Rapallo treaty, thus apparently implying that, once it was concluded, Soviet relations with Germany would be no more than on the same footing as Soviet relations with Poland. Nevertheless, economic relations continued to flourish, and as late as June 1932 a fresh credit agreement was negotiated in Moscow. In spite of quarrels and infidelities, mutual interest was still strong enough to keep the marriage in being.

The moment of Hitler's ascent to power is now approaching, and it is difficult for posterity to see the events of 1932 in any other light than as a prelude to that crowning catastrophe. Such hindsight was naturally denied to the politicians who shaped the events of the year. At Geneva the long and fruitless debates of the disarmament conference found Soviet and German delegates generally voting on the same side, though not always for exactly the same reasons. But when Brüning, the new German Chancellor and the first who frankly discarded parliamentary freedoms and ruled by presidential decree, visited Geneva in April 1932, another storm in a tea-cup showed the nervous and delicate state of German-Soviet friendship. It appears that Litvinov proposed a joint banquet to celebrate the tenth anniversary of the Rapallo treaty, at which speeches of mutual congratulations would be exchanged. Brüning on reflexion agreed to the banquet, but declined the speeches; and Litvinov retaliated by giving an interview full of barbed comment to the

German press. In July an agreement between Germany and the western Allies for a virtual cancellation of Germany's outstanding reparations debt was reached at Lausanne with the government of Von Papen, who had succeeded Brüning as Chancellor. This was read as a symptom of a further *rapprochement* between Germany and the west; and, when later in the same month the German delegation left the disarmament conference for the first time as a protest against its dilatory performance and its failure to recognize German equality of rights, the Soviet delegation continued to sit. At the same moment the Soviet-Polish non-aggression pact was signed in Warsaw. In November the long-awaited Franco-Soviet non-aggression pact was signed in Paris; and Litvinov was reported to be in negotiation with the Rumanian delegate in Geneva. Hatchets were being buried all round, and new safeguards sought for Soviet security some time before Hitler made his volte-face in foreign policy. In the last days of 1932 Seeckt, retired and embittered, wrote a pamphlet entitled *Germany between East and West*, in which he complained that German policy was pushing Russia into the arms of France. This pamphlet contained the remarkable prophecy that, if Germany ignored Russia, she would one day have Poland on the Oder.

In Germany the economic crisis was at its height and the bankruptcy of the Weimar republic was evident. But few people ventured to guess what would succeed it. It had come as a shock to the world when, at the Reichstag elections of September 1930 Adolf Hitler's hitherto insignificant National Socialist Party won 105 seats. It was a still greater shock when at the elections of July 1932

it won 230 seats. But what was even more noteworthy
was the changing outlook and status of the party. In
1930 Otto Strasser, the leader of its Left wing and the
champion of the socialist element in its original programme, had left it; and its evolution from this point
onwards was steadily towards unqualified nationalism and
the quest for power irrespective of programme or principle.
A corresponding change of attitude occurred among the
supporters of the old Right parties; they were no longer
willing, as they had been under Stresemann, to play the
game of parliamentary democracy in which they had never
believed, and gravitated easily towards the one party
which openly proposed to destroy it. The Right began to
disintegrate; Stresemann's German People's Party in particular, went into a rapid decline after his death in October
1929. It was these sources and from the unattached non-
political petty bourgeoisie that Hitler drew most of his new
recruits. The National Socialist Party lost the hybrid
character implied in its title, and became unequivocally
a party of the Right. A bargain was struck between Hitler
and Hugenberg, an industrial magnate and a member of
the German National Party, whose position as proprietor
of a vast newspaper and film syndicate gave him unique
opportunities as a political manipulator; and Hitler began
to receive large subsidies from industrial and financial
circles. The shape of the coming revolution was defining
itself. It was not understood only because Germany and
the world were obsessed by the idea that revolutions
always come from the Left.

During this period the other parties were in appearance
little affected. The Catholic Centre kept up its vote,

though it was paralysed by Brüning's ineffectual leadership and exercised no influence on the course of events. The German Social-Democratic Party barely held its ground, but even in November 1932 still polled over 7 million votes. The German Communist Party was the only party besides the Nazis to increase its vote. In the four-and-a-half years between May 1928 and November 1932 the number of its deputies in the Reichstag had almost doubled. In 1928 it polled just over 3 million votes, in July 1932 over 5 million and in November 1932 nearly 6 million, only a million behind the Social-Democrats. The highest Nazi vote in 1932 was 13,700,000 in July. In the light of these figures, it has often been said — first and most trenchantly by Trotsky — that an alliance between the Communists and Social-Democrats could have kept Hitler out, and that Moscow, by encouraging the German Communist Party in its intransigeant behaviour towards the Social-Democrats, helped Hitler to power. It is a good debating point. That the two great parties of the German Left should have spent their major energies in the year before Hitler's accession to power campaigning against one another is bound to seem both a tragedy and a crime, for which the German Communists, approved and abetted from the headquarters of Comintern, bear the main share of guilt. Some years later, at the seventh congress of Comintern, they were censured retrospectively for having at this time seen Fascism where it did not exist and failed to see it in its grossest form under their eyes. But in the actual conditions in Germany in 1932 the charge of responsibility for Hitler's rise to power is rather unreal. The German Social-Democratic Party had long ceased to believe in revolutionary methods; it was the only party which had unreservedly embraced the constitutional democracy of the Weimar republic. The German Communist Party remained in theory a revolutionary party, but since 1923 had been wedded to the belief, which was fully endorsed in Moscow, that the time was not ripe for revolution in Germany and that to resort to force was to court disaster; it had become a party of opposition and protest, but not of action, and had prospered as such. The essential fact in the Germany of 1932 was that Hitler intended to use force, if necessary, to overthrow the Weimar republic, and that no party which was unprepared to use force counted any longer in German politics. Had the German Social-Democrats and Communists formed a common front in the country and in the Reichstag, they might have compelled Hitler to apply openly illegal procedures rather earlier than he did. More they would scarcely have achieved by the non-violent methods to which they were both committed. Nor, even if they had been willing to use force in defence of Weimar, had they any reasonable hopes of success. The supreme arbiter, if it came to fighting, would be the Reichswehr; and experience had shown that the Reichswehr might tolerate violence from the Right, but never from the Left. Hitler, secure in the support of industry and finance, still moved cautiously so long as he had not received the green light from the Reichswehr. If the Left had moved, he would have received it at once.

The death agony of Weimar was unduly protracted. It is said, on rather dubious authority, that in the autumn of 1932 a spokesman of the Social-Democratic Party visited the Soviet Ambassador at Berlin, asked him to

promote a *rapprochement* between the Social-Democrats
and the Communists, and received a rebuff. In the November elections, which increased Communist representation
in the Reichstag from 89 to 100 and reduced Social-
Democratic representation from 143 to 121, the Nazis by
some odd electoral chance saw the number of their deputies
decline from 230 to 196. A sigh of relief went round
Europe: National Socialism had passed its zenith. A
government was formed under General von Schleicher who
at length realized his ambition to play a major role on the
political stage. The appointment was calculated to reas-
sure both the German Left and Soviet Russia. Schleicher
had inherited the Seeckt tradition. At home he was prepared to maintain the forms of parliamentary democracy
and to support measures of social reform, so long as the
status and authority of the Reichswehr were not impaired;
abroad he stood uncompromisingly for the Russian alliance. On both grounds he was no friend of the Nazis.
His appointment was a tribute to the commanding position
of the Reichswehr in the current political crisis. But it
soon transpired that Schleicher, who had neither Seeckt's
personality nor prestige, no longer enjoyed the unqualified
confidence of the Reichswehr and was unable to face the
hostility of the Right. In January 1933 Hindenburg broke
him, and conferred the Chancellorship on Hitler with a
coalition government which included Hugenberg. The decision meant that the Reichswehr was behind the new
combination and would endorse whatever measures it
thought necessary to take.

The outstanding consequence of the Nazi revolution in
the history of German-Soviet relations was Hitler's reversal

of the policy of Weimar towards Soviet Russia. As the
foregoing narrative has shown, many steps towards this
reversal had been taken long before Hitler came into
power, and it was not fully carried out till a year after
January 1933. It was therefore a far less sudden and
dramatic change than it is sometimes made to appear.
One point, however, now becomes obvious. From the
moment of Hitler's rise to power Germany was calling the
tune in German-Soviet relations, and the cooling off of
German-Soviet friendship came primarily from her side.
For the first few weeks of the new regime a certain
tendency existed on both sides to pretend that nothing
serious had happened. In March 1933 Göring gave a press
interview in which he explained that " our own campaign
for the extirpation of Communism in Germany has nothing
to do with German-Russian relations," which would, he
was convinced, " remain as friendly as in former years ";
and this attitude was confirmed by Hitler in his first foreign
policy speech on March 25. In May a protocol formally
renewing the half-forgotten neutrality pact of April 1926,
which had been signed in the spring of 1931, but left un-
ratified by successive German Governments, was duly
ratified; and *Izvestiya* seized the occasion to remark that
" in spite of their attitude towards Fascism, the people of
the USSR wish to live in peace with Germany and consider
that the development of German-Soviet relations is in the
interest of both countries."

This dual policy, however, soon became difficult to maintain. When the Reichstag fire touched off the first massive
explosion of abuse against Communists in general and
Comintern in particular, Litvinov is said to have asked

his German colleague at the disarmament conference in Geneva what these accusations meant, suggesting that they could only portend a change in German policy. For a long time Soviet reactions to the rising flood of invective in the utterances of the Führer and in the Nazi press remained unusually mild. As late as September 1933 at the session of the All-Union Central Executive Committee, Molotov cautiously observed that " the USSR has no reason to alter her policy towards Germany," though in Germany " many attempts have been made in the past year to revise relations with the Soviet Union "; and Litvinov dotted the i's of this policy with a rather crude avowal of Soviet opportunism:

> We of course sympathise with the sufferings of our German comrades, but we Marxists are the last who can be reproached with allowing our feelings to dictate our policy.
>
> The whole world knows that we can and do maintain good relations with capitalist states of any brand, including the Fascist. We do not interfere in the internal affairs of Germany, as we do not interfere in those of other countries; and our relations with her are conditioned not by her internal but by her external policy.

At this time the Soviet leaders were evidently still hoping against hope that Hitler's hatred of Communism did not imply hostility to Soviet Russia. But the decisive stroke was now not long delayed. On January 26, 1934, the German and Polish Governments recorded in a joint declaration their determination to effect " a peaceful development of their relations," and to settle their innumerable differences by direct negotiation. What this meant in practice was that Hitler was prepared to sacrifice the German population of Danzig and the German minority in Poland for the sake of a political alliance with Poland.

The fatal blow had been struck at the perennially sensitive point of German-Soviet friendship. The policy of Rapallo, the diplomacy of the Weimar republic, had been finally abandoned.

Hitler's decision to make this far-reaching change of front is the most puzzling and controversial in the story of German-Soviet relations. That the change was unwelcome to the leading Reichswehr generals, who remained secretly unreconciled to it throughout the nineteen-thirties, is well known. Rauschning, the Nazi President of the Free City of Danzig, records that it was highly unpopular in at any rate some party circles. Of the party leaders only Rosenberg was strongly anti-Russian; and he had hitherto never held an important place in the councils of the party. The diatribes of *Mein Kampf* and the ambitions of finding *Lebensraum* in the Ukraine remained. But so much in the original programme of National Socialism had been silently abandoned or relegated to a distant future that these could hardly be treated as a binding commitment. The initial pronouncements of the regime showed that, while the extirpation of Communism at home was a consistent aim from the moment of the seizure of power, the breach with Soviet Russia was not. The shifting balance of opinion in industrial and business circles may have been a contributory factor in the change. In financial circles opposition to the indulgence shown by the Weimar republic for Soviet Russia had been active ever since the granting of credits in 1926, when the German Government had intervened to moderate the exorbitant rate of interest demanded by the banks. After the British rupture of relations with Moscow in 1927 underground discussions seem to have been con-

ducted between a German group including Arnold Rechberg and Kühlmann, the former German Foreign Minister
and Trotsky's antagonist at Brest-Litovsk, and prominent
personalities in Great Britain on the basis of a return to
Germany of some of her former colonies and the abandonment of her economic relations with Soviet Russia. The
adoption of the first Soviet Five-Year Plan in October
1928 raised fresh doubts. The policy of the rapid large-
scale industrialization of Russia embodied in the plan
promised extensive orders to German heavy industry and
was valuable in this respect, especially during the years
of the acute economic crisis. On the other hand, as time
went on, more and more German industrialists began to
see in the Russia of the future, no longer a boundless
market or a rich source of raw materials, but a potential
industrial rival. One of the landmarks of the deterioration
of German-Soviet relations after Hitler's accession to power
was a memorandum circulated to the world economic
conference in London in the summer of 1933 by Hugenberg
which resuscitated in a thinly disguised form the old idea
of an international consortium to exploit the natural
resources of Russia and the Ukraine. In the present state
of evidence, it is impossible to assign a single or predominant motive to the change of front in German foreign
policy which reached its consummation in the German-
Polish agreement of January 1934. But this act, which
foreshadowed the declaration of war against Soviet Russia
in 1941, presents a remarkable parallel to William II's
refusal in 1890 to renew the German-Russian " reinsurance
treaty " of 1887 — the prelude to the war of 1914. Hitler
certainly acted against the advice of the Reichswehr

generals as William II had acted against that of Bismarck. In both cases the neglected warnings of those Germans who regarded friendly relations with Russia as a permanent and indispensable ingredient of German foreign policy were amply justified.

CHAPTER VI

HITLER AND STALIN

THE FIRST SOVIET response to growing fears of Hitler's attitude was to continue and strengthen the cautious movement of *rapprochement* with the west, especially at Geneva, which had been in progress before Hitler's rise to power. A few days after Hitler became Chancellor, Litvinov made a speech expressing sympathy with French demands for security, and put forward a draft convention for the definition of agression which met with more approval from France than from Germany or Great Britain. The signature at Rome in March 1933 of a four-Power pact between Great Britain, France, Germany and Italy, in which the possibility of invoking article 19 of the Covenant of the League of Nations to revise the peace treaties was delicately hinted at, provoked fresh mistrust in Moscow. France was known to be an unwilling and hesitant partner in the pact, and French objections were applauded by Soviet spokesmen, who were once more haunted by the vision of a western European combination potentially directed against Soviet Russia. The tone of the Soviet press underwent a slow and at first barely perceptible change. On March 30, 1933, *Izvestiya* wrote sympathetically of a speech of Mr. Churchill in the British House of Commons against treaty revision. In the summer

114

the same journal published a series of articles by Radek, which were subsequently republished in a pamphlet, on the theme that German pleas for the revision of Versailles were a prelude to a new imperialist partition of the world. The retirement of Germany from the League of Nations in October 1933 hastened a reconsideration of the traditional Soviet attitude of uncompromising hostility to that organization. On December 25, 1933, Stalin made a sensation by admitting in an interview given to an American correspondent, that the League might in certain cases act as a brake on the drift to war, and that Soviet reactions to it were not in all circumstances unconditionally hostile.

This was the situation when Hitler, in January 1934, aimed at German-Soviet friendship the final and fatal blow of the German-Polish agreement. From this point German-Soviet relations became on both sides openly unfriendly. A Soviet proposal for a Soviet-German pact guaranteeing the independence of the Baltic states was rejected in no uncertain terms when Litvinov visited Berlin — for the last time — in June 1934; and in the same month the recently appointed German Ambassador in Moscow, Nadolny, a diplomat long known for his advocacy of an eastern orientation in German foreign policy, resigned in protest against the new line. In September 1934 Soviet Russia joined the League of Nations and was elected a permanent member of the Council. During the next four years, Soviet Russia, regularly represented at Geneva by Litvinov, became the most active and loyal supporter of the League, loudly condemning every infringement of the sanctity of treaties, and demanding on all occasions the most rigorous application of the terms of the

Covenant and of sanctions against defaulters. " Collective security " and the " indivisibility of war " became the most popular themes of Soviet diplomacy and propaganda.

It was also necessary to gear the activities of Comintern in with the new line. No world congress had been held since 1928, when the doctrine of the united front had been abandoned and Social-Democrats denounced as " Social-Fascists." As late as December 1933, the executive committee of Comintern was hurling its anathemas against France; and at the Russian party congress of February of 1934 Manuilsky, reporting on the work of Comintern, reflected with satisfaction on the isolation of Germany who no longer had any friends. A year later this confident mood had completely changed. Fear followed self-congratulation; the cooperation of Social-Democrats of France and other countries was now urgently required. Hitler's announcement of what he called " the restoration of German sovereignty " and unlimited rearmament came in March 1935. It was followed at the beginning of May by the conclusion of a Franco-Soviet pact of mutual assistance, and two weeks later by a similar pact between Soviet Russia and Czechoslovakia, which bound Soviet Russia to come to the assistance of Czechoslovakia in the event of attack, provided France did likewise. After the signature of the Franco-Soviet pact a communiqué was issued in which Stalin gave his blessing to French rearmament. This was a signal to French Communists to abandon their old hostility to French armaments and to make common cause with other French parties of the Left. In July 1935 a congress of Comintern — the seventh and last — was summoned for the purpose of generalizing the new line which had been worked out in France. " In face of the towering menace of Fascism," declared the main resolution, " . . . it is the main and immediate task of the international labour movement in the present phase of history to establish the united fighting front of the working class." The workers of all countries were enjoined " to help with all their might and by all means to strengthen the USSR and the fight against the enemies of the USSR." The efforts of Communists to carry out this directive were a conspicuous feature of the political landscape in France, in Great Britain and even in the United States during the next few years.

The years 1936 and 1937 saw tension between Germany and Soviet Russia at its maximum. Normal relations between the two countries scarcely existed, and the speeches of Hitler and Goebbels in particular reached new heights of frenzy. The German denunciation of Locarno and the re-militarization of the Rhineland was justified on the ground of the Franco-Soviet pact which " introduces the military power of a mighty empire into the centre of Europe by the roundabout way of Czechoslovakia." Having explained that " Soviet Russia is the exponent of a revolutionary political and philosophic system organized in the form of a state," Hitler added by way of an afterthought:

> For purely territorial reasons alone Germany is not in a position to attack Russia; but Russia could at any time bring about a conflict with Germany by the indirect way of her advanced positions.

In July 1936 the outbreak of the Spanish Civil War offered fresh scope for the mutual enmity of the two Powers. In September at the Assembly of the League of Nations,

Litvinov branded " National Socialism and racism " as " deadly enemies of all the workers and of civilization itself." In November Germany and Japan signed the so-called " Anti-Comintern Pact " under which they agreed to concert measures together to counter the threat of Comintern. The essence of the pact resided in a secret addendum which equated Soviet Russia with Comintern. A year later, Hitler in the confidential address to his principal lieutenants, recorded in the so-called Hossbach memorandum which figured largely at the Nuremberg trial, counted on Japan to deter Soviet Russia from coming to the aid of Austria or Czechoslovakia.

By this time all Soviet Russia's international relations were being overshadowed by the most enigmatic episode, or series of episodes, of the period between the world wars — the state trials and the purges in Moscow. These began with the trial in August 1936 of Zinoviev, Kamenev and other members of what was called the " Trotskyite-Zinovievite Terrorist Centre "; the charges related to underground conspiracy against the Soviet regime, and the international element in them was secondary. The second trial of a " Trotskyite Anti-Soviet Centre," which included such well-known figures as Radek and Sokolnikov, took place in January 1937. This was immediately after the signing of the Anti-Comintern Pact, and the charges turned largely on alleged treasonable conspiracy with German and Japanese agents; Germany had been promised, among other things, the cession of the Ukraine. These trials were held in public and were characterized by the more or less complete confession of their guilt by all the accused. In June 1937 it was announced that Tukhachevsky, the Chief of Staff of the Red Army, and four other leading Soviet generals had been executed after a secret trial on charges of treason and espionage on behalf of foreign Powers. Finally in March 1938 Bukharin, Rykov, Krestinsky and other members of a so-called " Anti-Soviet Bloc of Rights and Trotskyites " were publicly tried on similar charges. Germany and Japan were still the principal countries aimed at.

Nobody outside Soviet Russia or the Communist Parties in other countries believed that all or most of the confessions made in these notorious trials were even approximately true. Of serious critics, some would dismiss them as totally false; others would point out that underground opposition activities indubitably went on in Soviet Russia during those years, that secret agents of foreign Powers unquestionably operated there, and that there is no *a priori* reason why some of the defendants should not have been engaged in conspiracy against the regime, whether with or without foreign backing. This is not the place to attempt any general evalution of the trials. But a few comments may be offered on their relation to German-Soviet relations. Radek at his trial was not required to testify on the role played by him in Germany in the early 1920's. At that time he was acting mainly as the agent of Comintern and of the Russian Communist Party; and neither Comintern nor party affairs were brought into the trials at any point. The charges brought against Radek were confined to the period after 1932 and included none of direct contact with the German Government. At the later trial, on the other hand, Krestinsky, as was noted in a previous chapter, was closely examined on the secret negotiations with the Reichswehr from 1921 onwards, and the arrangements made as the result of these negotiations were treated as a Trotskyite conspiracy. The generals executed after the secret trial of June 1937, all of whom occupied prominent posts in the 1920's, had certainly been concerned in these arrangements; their share in them may have been the basis of the charges against the generals, as it was against Krestinsky. One of the most circumstantial of the accounts published before 1939 appeared in the German military journal *Deutsche Wehr* in October 1938. According to this version Tukhachevsky's project of a coup against Stalin dated back to 1935; it was fixed to take place in May 1937 and was betrayed at the last moment by Skoblin, a " white " Russian general living in Paris who was presumably on this hypothesis an agent of the NKVD.

The end of the second world war released a flood of contradictory stories about the trials, but no shred of documentary evidence. The Red Army leaders, nourished in a long tradition of congenial cooperation with the Reichswehr, probably disliked the breach of relations as much as did the leading Reichswehr generals. It is conceivable that relations were maintained between them behind the backs of the two dictators after the official rupture. Elements in the Reichswehr which would have liked to get rid of Hitler may possibly have exchanged ideas with officers of the Red Army who had similar ideas about Stalin. This hypothesis, plausible in itself, fits in with the story told by Benes to Winston Churchill in 1944 and recorded in Churchill's memoirs. According to this story, the Czech secret service discovered that communica-

tions were passing through Prague " between important per-
sonages in Russia and the German Government "; these
related to " an old-guard Communist conspiracy to overthrow Stalin and introduce a new regime based on a pro-
German policy "; and Benes lost no time in communicating
this information to Stalin. A more refined account, which
seems to conform best with the principle *cui bono?*,
describes how the documents compromising the Red Army
generals were communicated by Heydrich to the Soviet
authorities in the hope of discrediting and destroying the
generals — a plot which succeeded beyond all expectations: those who tell this story differ as to whether the
documents were genuine documents dating from the period
of cooperation between the two armies or were forged by
Heydrich for the occasion. A more refined version still
maintains that the compromising documents were forged
by the NKVD and planted in such a way as to make it
appear that they emanated from German sources. The
student of history is still without any serious evidence
which would enable him to confirm or deny any of these
picturesque and conflicting accounts.

The most important international consequence of the
trials and of the widespread purge which accompanied
them was to lower the prestige of Soviet Russia and to
confound those abroad who had preached cooperation
with the Soviet Government as the way to counter German
aggression. Whether the charges were true or false, the
mere fact of the trials and of the execution of so many
notables, military and civilian, seemed to reveal a society
and an army so rotten, and so fundamentally divided
against themselves, that it was difficult to believe in

Soviet Russia as an effective ally against German military power. The forces in other countries which sought to come to terms with Germany were correspondingly strengthened. These effects became apparent during the winter of 1937-1938, when the stage was already being set for the last act in the drama. Four months before the last of the Soviet trials, on November 5, 1937, Hitler, as is now known from the Hossbach memorandum, had cast the die for war. At the same time the policy of appeasement passed from its passive into its active phase. In the summer of 1937 Neville Chamberlain succeeded Baldwin as British Prime Minister. In the middle of November, ten days after Hitler's announcement of his decision to his generals, Lord Halifax visited Hitler and Ribbentrop in Germany. In February 1938, Eden resigned and was succeeded by Halifax at the Foreign Office. The effect of these changes on German-Soviet relations was complex, unforeseen, and crucial.

In Germany, Hitler had succeeded to a remarkable extent in dividing the Reichswehr against itself and curbing its authority. Paradoxically, the generals exercised far less political power in the Germany of Hitler than in the supposedly democratic Germany of Stresemann. Nor was this merely because Brauchitsch and Blomberg and Keitel were men of smaller stature than Seeckt and Hindenburg; it was also because Hitler was able to base his power on a far larger measure of popular support than the Weimar republic had ever enjoyed. Nevertheless, the decision to make war increased Hitler's dependence on the generals. On issues of war, so long as the Reichswehr spoke with a united voice, it was difficult to override its opinion.

It is probable that a majority of the generals preferred to fight the west with the support of Soviet Russia rather than come to terms with the west in order to fight the east. But this choice lay in Hitler's hands. The point on which the Reichswehr was unanimous and could still impose its decision on Hitler was its refusal to fight on both fronts at once. The choice one way or the other had to be made. Hitler disliked having to make it. On this issue he continued to hesitate for nearly eighteen months after Novermber 1937.

In Soviet Russia, though the decision of November 1937 remained of course unknown, it had been an axiom since 1935 that Hitler would start a war somewhere in Europe. The bugbear of Soviet statesmen was that it might be a war between Hitler and Soviet Russia with the western Powers neutral or tacitly favourable to Hitler. In order to conjure this bugbear one of two main alternatives had to be envisaged: either a war against Germany in which Soviet Russia would be allied with the western Powers, or a war between Germany and the western Powers in which Soviet Russia would remain neutral or tacitly favorable to Germany. It is fundamental to an understanding of Soviet policy at this time that the Soviet leaders thought an aggressive war by Hitler certain, and were determined at all costs to avoid having to face Hitler alone. If the alliance with the west failed, then neutrality in a war between Germany and the west, or at the worst alliance with Hitler, were the only ways out. The first alternative — alliance with the west against Hitler — had been forced on the Soviet leaders by Hitler's implacable hostility rather than spontaneously chosen by them.

But, once adopted, this line was consistently pursued from 1934 to 1938, both through the League of Nations and through specific pacts such as those with France and Czechoslovakia. At intervals during this time — and particularly in the first half of 1937 when the purges were at their height — circumstantial rumours circulated of approaches made to Hitler by secret emissaries of Stalin in the hope of healing the breach. Nothing to confirm these rumours has been found in any German documents captured in 1945; and, if such approaches occurred, they did not deflect the main line of Soviet policy.

What caused a change of atmosphere to set in during 1938 was the growth of doubts as to the willingness of the western Powers to enter into effective alliance with Soviet Russia. The vacillations of the west in face of Mussolini's aggression against Abyssinia and Hitler's coup in the Rhineland created in Moscow exactly the same impression of weakness as they created in Berlin. Developments in Great Britain during the winter of 1937-1938 intensified these fears which received their fullest confirmation in the Munich crisis of September 1938. At the height of the crisis a leading article in *Pravda* — the first for many weeks on foreign affairs — struck almost casually in its last prargraph a new note:

> The Soviet Union examines with composure the question which particular imperialist robber stretches out his hand for this or that colony or vassal state; for it sees no difference between German and English robbers. But the ' democratic ' states in western Europe cannot regard these questions with indifference. In consenting to the dismemberment of Czechoslovakia, in blessing this dismemberment, England and France are playing with fire.

To see " no difference between English and German

robbers " was the first hint of a potential shift from a
policy of cooperation with the west to a policy of neutrality
— a reversion to the old habit of regarding all imperialist
Powers as equally wicked. Having dropped this barely
audible hint, the Soviet press returned to its advocacy of
a common front against Hitler, and approvingly quoted
Litvinov's speech at the League of Nations in which be
had declared that Soviet Russia would fulfill her obligations
" in all ways available to us " — a hint at the opposition
of Poland and Rumania to the passage of Soviet forces
across their territiories. Then on September 29, 1938, the
Munich agreement was concluded without further consultation with Soviet Government. No overt move was made.
But the chagrin felt in Moscow was not concealed, and the
conclusions were left to ripen.

Thus, at a time when Hitler was still undecided whether
to move first against the east or against the west, and was
bound to weigh the contingency, if he decided to move
west, of having to patch up his tattered relations with
Soviet Russia, Soviet Russia was also being driven to con-
template the apparent bankruptcy of her western policy
and the necessity, if this were confirmed, of coming to
terms with Hitler. It is a tribute to the depth and tenacity
of the ill feeling between the two countries that it took so
long to bridge the gulf between them. The denunciations
of Bolshevism in Hitler's Nuremberg speech in September
1938 were far less vitriolic than those of the previous year.
After Munich, Hitler's increasingly bitter references to the
west were matched by a corresponding diminution of
acrimony, quantitive and qualitative, in regard to Soviet
Russia. In October 1938 Schulenburg, the German Am-

bassador in Moscow, apparently on his own initiative, suggested an agreement to keep the names and personalities of Hitler and Stalin out of the mutual press polemics; and both sides rather unexpectedly agreed to this. The prelude to the events of the spring and summer of 1939 was a speech by Stalin at the party congress on March 10th, 1939. This speech was an extraordinarily astute exercise in political tight-rope walking, from which it would be rash to draw any confident conclusion other than the indeterminate and embarrassed state of Soviet foreign policy at the time. Only about one-sixth of the whole speech was devoted to the subject, but the passage was placed at the beginning of the speech to indicate its importance. Stalin began by stating that an imperialist war was already in progress, and naming Japan, Germany and Italy as aggressors:

The three aggressive states and the imperialist war started by them have turned upside down the whole system of the post-war regime. . . . The aggressor states carry on war everywhere injuring the interests of the non-aggressive states, primarily England, France and the U. S. A., and the latter give ground and retreat, making one concession after another to the aggressors.

This attack on the aggressors was, however, carefully balanced by an attack on England and France, whose abandonment of collective security in favour of " non-intervention " and " neutrality " was, in Stalin's words, tantamount to saying: " Let every country defend itself against the aggressor as it will and can, our interest is not at stake, we shall bargain both with the aggressors and with their victims." This was " something very like encouragement of the aggressor," and was equal to saying to Germany: "Start a war with the Bolsheviks and all will be well." Stalin concluded the foreign policy section of his speech by laying down four tasks for the party:

(1) To carry out and continue a policy of peace and strengthening commercial relations with all countries;
(2) To observe caution and not to allow our country to be drawn into war by war-mongers who are accustomed to "rake the fire with other people's hands";
(3) By all means to strengthen the fighting powers of our Red Army and Red Fleet;
(4) To strengthen the international ties of friendship with the workers of all countries who are interested in peace and friendship between nations.

In spite of a divergence in the Russian idiom, the second of these items contained an obvious echo of the current American accusation against Great Britain of expecting others to "pull her chestnuts out of the fire for her"; this was its main significance.

Statesmen, like private individuals, sometimes betray the subconscious processes of their own minds by the motives which they attribute to others. In retrospect the most striking sentence in the speech was perhaps the one in which Stalin summed up his diagnosis of the attitude of the western Powers: "Let every country defend itself against the aggressor as it will and can, our interest is not at stake, we shall bargain with the aggressors and with their victims." Stalin's speech of March 10th, 1939, clearly did not announce any positive decision of Soviet policy; what it did was to keep all options open and to hint more plainly than before that they were open. Five days after the speech Hitler occupied Prague; and on March 18th, 1939, encouraged no doubt by the more vigorous reaction of British opinion and (after two days' hesitation) of the British Government to this coup, the Soviet Government handed to the German Ambassador in Moscow an exceedingly strong note, which was published, protesting against the German action and refusing to recognize the incorporation of the Czech lands in the Reich. Some tentative exchanges now occurred between the Soviet and British Governments. But a Soviet proposal for an immediate conference of the anti-Fascist Powers at Bukharest to concert military measures was rejected by Great Britain; and a British proposal for a pact between Great Britain, France, Soviet Russia and Poland for mutual consultation in the event of an act of aggression, though accepted by Moscow, was rejected by Poland. A British minister, who was in Moscow at the time for trade talks, declined to enter into any political discussions. Then on March 31, 1939, without any further approach to the Soviet Government, Great Britain gave to Poland a unilateral guarantee to come to her assistance if she were attacked. In the circumstances, the Soviet Government could hardly fail to deduce that Great Britain preferred the Polish to the Soviet alliance, and desired, as at Munich, to keep Soviet Russia out of major discussions affecting the peace of Europe.

The first formal step towards a Soviet *rapprochement* with Germany came a fortnight later in the form of an interview of the Soviet Ambassador in Berlin, Merekalov, with the German State-Secretary, Weizsäcker, on April 17th, 1939. Having discussed a routine question, Merekalov led the conversation to political matters and, after some beating about the bush, bluntly asked Weizsäcker what he thought of German-Russian relations. Weizsäcker cautiously observed that " the Russian press was not fully participating in the anti-German tone of the American and some of the English papers " and hinted at a similar restraint in the German press in regard to Russia. Thus encouraged Merekalov made the following statement:

Russian policy had always moved in a straight line. Ideological differences of opinion had hardly influenced the Italian-Russian relationship, and they did not have to prove a stumbling block with regard to Germany either. Soviet Russia had not exploited the present friction between Germany and the western democracies against us, nor did she desire to do so. There exists for Russia no reason why she should not live with us on a normal footing. And from normal, the relations might become better and better.

This rather clumsy confidential approach was followed by an exchange of public gestures. The first sign came in Hitler's speech of April 28, 1939, which was devoted to an attack on Poland; contrary to custom, it contained no word of abuse of Bolshevism or of Russia. The significance of this omission was underlined some days later by a prominent Nazi to a member of the French Embassy; and it seems not unlikely that a similar hint had already been conveyed to the Soviet Embassy by way of rejoinder to the *démarche* of April 17, 1939. The answer followed promptly. On May 3, 1939, Litvinov resigned the office of People's Commissar for Foreign Affairs and was succeeded by Molotov. Litvinov had been closely associated with the policy of collective security and was a Jew. The sudden decision, as officials correctly proclaimed, did not in itself herald a change of policy. Since Stalin's speech of March 10, 1939, had made it clear that two options were open, the presence at the head of Narkomindel of a com-

missar so publicly and conspicuously committed to one of
them had become an anomaly; in this sense the change was
a gesture of friendliness to Germany. Lest its significance
be lost, Astakhov, the Soviet chargé d'affaires in Berlin, in
the words of a German report, "tried without asking
questions to learn" from the German Foreign Office on
May 5 "whether this event would cause a change in our
position towards the Soviet Union."

The next three months — May, June and July — saw
the forefront of the stage occupied by the increasingly
involved and difficult Soviet negotiations with Britain
and France, negotiations with Germany being relegated
to the twilight of secret diplomacy in the background.
They advanced with a slowness which testified to the depth
of mutual suspicion. On May 20, 1939, the new Commissar
for Foreign Affairs received the German Ambassador for
the first time. After a discussion about economic affairs,
Molotov observed that "the Soviet Government could
only agree to a resumption of the [economic] negotiations
if the necessary 'political bases' for them had been constructed." Schulenburg, having tried in vain to probe what
lay behind these words, took his leave: "Herr Molotov
had apparently determined to say just so much and no
more." The German Foreign Office, apprised of this conversation, replied on the following day that "we must now
sit tight and wait to see if the Russians will speak more
openly." It soon transpired, however, that Molotov's taci-
turnity had won the first round of this waiting game. At
a conference on May 23, 1939, disclosed at the Nuremberg
trials, Hitler announced his intention "to attack Poland
at the first suitable opportunity"; and into the next few

days we can now fit an episode described by Gaus, legal adviser to the German Foreign Office, in his Nuremberg affidavit. Gaus and Weizsäcker were summoned to Ribbentrop's country house, and informed that Hitler wanted " to establish more tolerable relations between Germany and the USSR." Some pretext should be found in the way of current affairs to explore the possibility of political talks: it was decided to use for this purpose the question of Soviet consular representation in Prague. Draft instructions to Schulenburg were prepared, but when submitted to Hitler were found to be " too explicit." His hesitations were apparently due to Chamberlain's highly optimistic statement in the House of Commons on May 24 that agreement on essentials had been reached between Soviet Russia and the western Powers. A rebuff was now feared, and a more cautious approach decided on. On May 30, 1939, Weizsäcker sent for Astakhov and, after broaching the questions of the Prague consulate and the economic negotiations, expressed agreement with " Herr Molotov " that " politics and economics could not be entirely separated in our relations," reverted to the Soviet Ambassador's remarks in April about the " normalization and even further improvement of German-Russian political relations," and, having " changed over to a purely conversational tone," remarked *inter alia* that " the development of our relations with Poland . . . had actually made our hitherto restricted policy in the east freer." So far as the records show, this would-be subtle approach produced no visible effect. For a month discussions with Germany about economic negotiations proceeded without results. In interviews with Molotov on June 29 and July 3

Schulenburg still struggled in vain to secure from the costive commissar some amplification of his phrase of May 20 about " political bases." At the first of these conversations Molotov was particularly spiky; a reference by Schulenburg to Germany's non-aggression treaties with the Baltic states provoked the retort that " he had to doubt the permanence of such treaties after the experience which Poland had had." The impression left by these records is partly of a holding back for tactical reasons but also partly of a profound and ineradicable mistrust of German policy in the minds of the Soviet leaders.

It was not till the end of July that the ice began to melt; and this was plainly connected on the Soviet side with the deadlock in the political negotiations with Britain and France and the visit to London of a German economic commission headed by Wohltat. On July 22 it was announced that Soviet-German trade negotiations had been resumed in Berlin. The Germans now decided to speak more frankly, but through an informal channel. Schnurre, the German trade expert, was instructed to invite Astakhov and Babanin, the head of the Soviet trade delegation, to dinner; and the conversation, which took place on July 27, ranged far. For the first time the alternative was clearly put:

What could England offer Russia? At best, participation in a European war and the hostility of Germany, but not a single desirable end for Russia. What could we offer on the other hand? Neutrality and staying out of a possible European conflict, and if Moscow wished, a German-Russian understanding on mutual interests which, just as in former times, would work out to the advantage of both countries.

Three days later Weizsäcker in an instruction to Schulenburg added some further precision:

In any development of the Polish question, either in a peaceful manner as we desire it or in any other way that is forced on us, we would be prepared to safeguard all Soviet interests and to reach an understanding with the Moscow government. If the talk proceeds positively in the Baltic question too, the idea could be advanced that we will adjust our stand with regard to the Baltic in such a manner as to respect the vital Soviet interests in the Baltic.

Thus armed, Schulenburg had a conversation on August 3 with Molotov, who seems to have spoken most fully and eloquently on Germany's support of " the aggressive attitude of Japan towards the Soviet Union." An undeclared frontier war in the Far East between Soviet Russia and Japan had been in progress since May 1939, and had a substantial influence on the Soviet-German negotiations. If the avoidance of a war on two fronts was the compelling motive of the Germans in the *rapprochement* with Russia, it was also constantly present in the thoughts of the Soviet negotiators. Schulenburg's summary of the situation after the conversation was as follows:

My overall impression is that the Soviet Government is at present determined to sign with England and France if they fulfil all Soviet wishes. Negotiations, to be sure, might still last a long time, especially since mistrust of England is still great. I believe that my statements made an impression on M.; it will nevertheless take a considerable effort on our part to cause the Soviet Government to swing about.

But by this time the race between the two bidders for Soviet friendship had become altogether uneven; the impression could not be avoided at Moscow that one side was trying very hard and the other side not trying at all. This impression was merely strengthened by the undistinguished galaxy of military, naval and air talent which constituted the Anglo-French military mission, and by their choice of the slow sea route for their journey to

Moscow — which seemed yet another public demonstration of a fundamental lack of interest on the British side. The military conversations began on August 12 and proceeded uneventfully till, on the third day, Voroshilov punctured the whole pretence by openly raising the unsolved question — the hidden crux of the whole negotiation — of the passage of Soviet troops across Polish territory in the event of German aggression, adding that it was useless to continue the discussions till that was settled. This move was clearly intended as a sign-off. On August 12 Astakhov in Berlin had conveyed the agreement of the Soviet Government to a conference in Moscow to discuss Soviet-German relations; and two days later Ribbentrop telegraphed his own readiness to come to Moscow. " An extended conference with Stalin " was the only condition laid down.

With the game in the bag, the Soviet Government could afford to keep the Germans on the doorstep; and the last stages still betray a strong element of mistrust in Moscow. After a further exhibition of the hedging and stalling in which Molotov was a master, the Soviet Government on August 19 agreed to a visit " one week after the proclamation of the signing of the economic agreement." This was still too slow for the German military programme. Impatience at Berlin was expressed in a shower of telegrams and a personal message of August 20 from the Führer to " Herr Stalin," begging that " my Foreign Minister " should be received on August 22 or at the latest on August 23. Thus pressed Stalin accepted the second date. Ribbentrop arrived in Moscow on August 23, and the non-aggression pact and secret protocol were signed the same evening.

The protocol fixed the division between Soviet and German spheres of influence " in the event of a territorial and political transformation of these areas," in the Baltic states along the northern frontier of Lithuania (Molotov particularly stressed Soviet interest in the ice-free ports of Windau and Libau, and Hitler was consulted by telephone before agreement was given) and in Poland along the line of the Narew, Vistula and San; the Soviet Government affirmed its interest, the German Government its " political disinterestedness," in Bessarabia. On the next day Ribbentrop returned to Berlin. The British and French military missions bowed themselves out of Moscow thirty-six hours later; and on August 27 Molotov pronounced to the French Ambassador his obituary on the negotiations:

> The Soviet Government, having found that, in spite of the efforts of the three governments, the obstinate refusal of Poland made impossible a tripartite pact of mutual assistance, had for its part to settle the question by concluding a non-aggression pact with Germany. . . . A great country like the USSR could not beg Poland to accept help which she did not want at any price.

In his speech to the Supreme Soviet on August 31st, 1939, Molotov also named Polish objections as the chief cause of the breakdown. On the next day the German assault on Poland, and with it the second world war, began.

It remains to draw a few guarded conclusions from the story. The essential aim of Soviet foreign policy at this time was to avoid isolation: an understanding with one or other of the rival capitalist groups was a condition of Soviet security. By August 1939 the Soviet leaders had finally convinced themselves that the Chamberlain government, whose attitude dominated that of France, was irrevocably opposed to effective co-operation with Soviet

Russia. It desired to prevent the further expansion of Germany, but saw in this a lesser evil than a victory which would increase Soviet power. It refused therefore to enter into an alliance with Soviet Russia against Germany — appeasement at Munich, the preference given to Poland in March 1939, and the delays and hesitations of the summer of 1939 were treated as proofs of this refusal; and the calculation was that, if Hitler could not be restrained by diplomatic gestures, then he must be encouraged to turn against the east, the immunity of the west being purchased by open tacit support of aggression eastwards. Once this diagnosis of western policy had been accepted in Moscow, only one conclusion could be drawn: if the western alliance could not be achieved, then let Hitler at all costs strike west and let Russia purchase immunity by " non-intervention." This was the conception embodied in the pact of August 23, 1939, when in return for " non-intervention " Stalin secured a breathing space of immunity from German attack, German assistance in mitigating Japanese pressure in the Far East, and German agreement to the establishment of an advanced defensive bastion beyond the existing Soviet frontiers in eastern Europe; it was significant that this bastion was, and could only be, a line of defence against potential German attack, the eventual prospect of which was never absent from Soviet reckonings. But what most of all was achieved by the pact was the assurance that, if Soviet Russia had eventually to fight Hitler, the western Powers would already be involved, and could no longer escape by shifting the brunt of the attack on to Russia. The final justification found by the official Soviet *History of Diplomacy* for the " diplomacy of Stalin " is that "at the moment of the most intense struggle with the enemy the Soviet Union did not stand alone."

For Germany the moral of the pact of August 23, 1939, and of the story of German-Soviet relations over the past twenty years was simpler and less equivocal. The diplomatic recovery, and in part also the military recovery, of Germany after the disaster of 1918 had been achieved through a policy of friendship and cooperation with Soviet Russia which made it possible to play off the east against the west. When Hitler was tempted to break with Russia in 1934, Germany was isolated and German foreign policy ran into a dead-end, from which there was no escape till, after an aberration lasting five years, Hitler once more came to terms with Soviet Russia and regained his freedom of action against the west. This was the significance for Germany of the German-Soviet pact. "What has been desired since 1870 and regarded as impossible of achievement," said Hitler boastfully to his military commanders in November 1939, "has come to pass. For the first time in history we have to fight only on one front." So long as that situation was maintained, German fortunes prospered. But less than two years later Hitler was tempted and fell, repeating the blunder of William II and courting war against the country on whose cooperation or friendly neutrality German military success had always depended. The question-mark which confronts the world little more than ten years after the close of this story is whether German leaders, once more in possession of the means to conduct a German foreign policy, would be content for a third time to reject the policy of Bismarck and the advice of the most successful of their monarchs to " cultivate the friendship of these barbarians."

NOTE ON SOURCES

The best political history of Germany under the Weimar republic is still perhaps Arthur Rosenberg, *A History of the German Republic* (English transl. 1936); the author was a former member of the German Communist Party. F. Stampfer, *Die Ersten Vierzehn Jahre der Deutschen Republik* (1947), is written from the standpoint of the German Social-Democratic Party, the author having been editor of the principal party newspaper *Vorwärts*. O. K. Flechtheim, *Die KPD in der Weimarer Republik* (1948) is a careful study of its subject, often throwing side-lights on German-Soviet relations.

The debates of the Reichstag are an important source throughout the Weimar period. No official German documents for this period have yet been published; *Documents on British Foreign Policy 1919-1939: First Series*, Vol. iii (1949) contains useful reports on events in Germany and in the Baltic in 1919.

The personal records of Seeckt and Stresemann, of both of which only a part has yet been published, contain material of outstanding importance for German-Soviet relations:—

F. von Rabenau, *Seeckt: Aus Seinem Leben 1918-1936* (1941), like a previous volume on Seeckt's earlier career published in 1938, was based on Seeckt's personal archives, and, though naturally selective, told in outline for the first time the story of the secret German-Soviet military arrangements from 1921 onwards. A few other important documents from, or relating to, the Seeckt archives were printed in *Der Monat* Vol. I. No. 2 (November 1948); and an account of further unpublished papers of Seeckt and others from the German military archives is given by G. W. F. Hallgarten in *The Journal of Modern History*, vol. XXI, No. 1 (March 1949).

Gustav Stresemann: His Diaries, Letters and Papers (Engl. transl. 3 vols. 1935-1940) is a primary source for German foreign policy in the years 1923-1929, though being designed to build up a picture of

Stresemann as a " westerner " it is least satisfactory in its account of
his eastern policy: Professor Sontag, who has seen the mass of
unpublished Stresemann papers from which this selection was made,
has testified that they contain evidence of Stresemann's knowledge
and approval of the German-Soviet secret military arrangements
(*American Historical Review*, Vol. LV, No. 3 (April 1950) p. 738).

H. Kessler, *Walther Rathenau: His Life and Work* (Engl. transl.
1930) is an important source for the signature of the Rapallo treaty.
It makes no mention of Rathenau's contacts with Radek in 1919, or
of the secret German-Soviet military arrangements, of which he was
certainly cognisant. The ideas expressed by Rathenau to Radek find
general confirmation in his essays *Kritik der Dreifachen Revolution,
Die Neue Wirtschaft* and *Von Kommenden Dingen*, and in a letter of
1912 quoted in Kessler's biography, p. 266.

C. F. Melville, *The Russian Face of Germany* (1932) contains
particulars of the Social-Democratic disclosures of secret German-
Soviet military cooperation; V. N. Ipatieff, *The Life of a Chemist*
(Stanford 1946) describes attempts to produce poison gas.

D'Abernon, *The Diary of an Ambassador* [in English edition, *An
Ambassador of Peace*] (3 vols. 1929-1931), contains the diary of the
British Ambassador for the period, but, in spite of much detail, is a
disappointing source for German-Soviet relations, on which D'Abernon
was poorly informed.

Incidental information may be found in the numerous published
memoirs of German generals and politicians, notably in those of Max
von Baden, Ludendorff, Max Hoffmann, Max Bauer, Emil Barth and
Philip Scheidemann. Ruth Fischer, *Stalin and German Communism*
(1948), provides first-hand, but not unbiassed, information on the
relations of the German Communist Party with Moscow.

No serious attempt has yet been made to write a history of
Germany under Hitler. *Hitler's Speeches*, ed. N. H. Baynes (2 vols.
1942), is a useful classified collection of extracts from major political
utterances.

Nazi-Soviet Relations 1939-1941 (Department of State, Washington,
D. C., 1948) is a selection of documents from the German archives to
illustrate the Nazi-Soviet *rapprochement* of 1939 and its sequel.
Neither the collection of German nor of British official documents in

course of publication is yet available for this period: the volumes of both collections for the period preceding Munich throw little light on German-Soviet relations.

The official records of the Nuremberg trials of war criminals, down to and including the Krupp trial, contain occasional sidelights on German-Soviet relations for the period before 1939; in view of their vast bulk, and the comparative inaccessibility of the later records, they have not yet been fully sifted and utilized by scholars.

Among a flood of memoirs by German generals and officials published since 1945 the most informative on the subject are two written by former members of the German diplomatic service: Erich Kordt, *Wahn und Wirklichkeit* (1948), and Herbert von Dirksen, *Moskau-Tokio-London* (n. d. [1950]).

* * * * * * * *

Among Soviet works the third volume of the semi-official *Istoriya Diplomatii* purports to cover the period but is virtually useless for present purposes; published in 1945, when everything German was anathema in Moscow, it casts over every aspect of German-Soviet relations a veil so opaque as to obliterate everything but a few bare facts. The contemporary Soviet view of these relations in the nineteen-twenties is given in A. Erusalimsky, *Germaniya, Antanta i SSSR* (1928).

The best general account of Soviet foreign policy up to 1929 is L. Fischer, *The Soviets in World Affairs* (2 vols. 1930); the author was in close touch with leading Soviet personalities, including Chicherin. Max Beloff, *The Foreign Policy of Soviet Russia 1929-1941* (2 vols. 1947, 1949), begins where Fischer leaves off, and provides a detailed and well documented narrative, though he soon reaches a period where speculation is required to supplement knowledge.

The specialist student will still have to consult the original Russian sources, including the records of the congresses of Comintern and sessions of its executive, of the congresses of the Russian (later All-Union) Communist Party, of the All-Russian (later All-Union) Congress of Soviets, and of the All-Russian (later All-Union) Central Executive Committee. Relevant speeches and writings of Lenin, Stalin, Litvinov and Molotov are available in many editions and in several languages. A valuable guide to these, as well as to collections of official documents and important press articles, is the

Calendar of Soviet Documents on Foreign Policy compiled by Jane Degras (Royal Institute of International Affairs 1948). The first volume of a comprehensive selection of *Soviet Documents on Foreign Policy* by the same editor (Oxford University Press 1951) appeared too late for use in the present work.

The memoirs of Radek quoted in chapter I are in *Krasnaya Nov'*, October (No. 10), 1926. According to an article by B. Nikolaevsky in *Novyi Zhurnal*, No. 1 (N. Y. 1942), p. 244, these memoirs were reprinted as a pamphlet in the following year with the omission of the passage relating to Radek's conversations with German notabilities; Nikolaevsky is, however, wrong in describing the moment of the original publication of these reminiscences (October 1926) as one of particular tension in Soviet-German relations. Radek also wrote between 1919 and 1923 a large number of political pamphlets, most of them originally published in German.

The unpublished Trotsky archives quoted in Chapter III are in the Widener Library at Harvard; I am indebted for my references to these archives to Mr. Isaac Deutscher, author of *Stalin: A Political Biography* (1949), who generously placed his notes of them at my disposal.

Letters of Krasin are quoted from Lyubov Krasin, *Leonid Krasin: The Man and his Work* (n. d. [1929]).

Many books published by émigrés from the USSR contain sensational stories about secret German-Soviet relations, especially in the nineteen-thirties; but these frequently contradict one another and are still unsubstantiated by serious evidence.

INDEX

Albatrosswerke: 57
America (American): *see* United States
Anglo-Soviet Trade Agreement: 40–41, 46, 51
Anti-Comintern Pact: 118
Astakhov: 130–132, 134

Babanin: 132
Baldwin, Earl: 122
Barthou: 63
Bauer, Max: 20, 22, 37
Bela Kun: 44
Benes, Eduard: 120
Berendt: 62
Berliner Tageblatt: 94
Berlin Treaty (1926): 87, 109
Bismarck: 1, 34, 86–87, 113, 137
Blöhm and Voss: 57
Blomberg, Field-Marshall: 30, 122
Brandler: 72, 74–75
Brauchitsch, General: 122
Brazil: 86
Brest-Litovsk Treaty: 2–3, 18, 21, 26, 41, 49
Britain (British): *see* Great Britain
Brockdorff-Rantzau: 67–68, 76, 84, 93, 101
Brüning: 103–104, 106
Brusilov: 38
Bukharin, Nikolai: 3, 43, 72, 97, 119

Centre Party, German: 7, 105
Chamberlain, Austen: 96
Chamberlain, Neville: 122, 131, 135
Chiang Kai-shek: 98
Chicherin: 26–27, 54, 57, 63, 66, 68–69, 81–86, 91, 94, 97
China: 97–99

Churchill, Winston: 114, 120
Clemenceau: 8–9
Comintern: *see* Communist International
Communist International (Comintern): 26–27, 33–34, 38, 41–44, 46–47, 65, 69–72, 76, 97–100, 106, 109, 116
Communist Party, British: 98
Communist Party, Chinese: 98
Communist Party, French: 116
Communist Party, German: 7–10, 17, 20, 22, 27–29, 33, 42–46, 69–74, 76–77, 82, 85, 87, 94, 99, 106–108, 119
Communist Party, Russian (*later* All-Union): 8, 23, 38, 97, 99, 116, 119
Cuno, Hans: 70, 71
Curtius, Ernst: 102
Czecho-Slovakia: 116–17, 120, 124, 128

D'Abernon, Viscount: 17, 57, 62, 65, 87
Danzig: 35, 110
Dawes Plan: 77, 79, 81–82, 85, 91
Deutsche Wehr: 120
Deutsch, Felix: 20, 68
Dirksen, Herbert von: 101
Disarmament Conference: 110

Ebert: 10, 11 n., 67
Eden, Anthony: 122
Enver: 18, 22, 36–67, 56 n.
Estonia: 14

Five-Year Plan: 100, 112
Foch, Marshal: 70
France: 53, 60, 70–71, 75, 77, 80, 86, 102, 104, 114, 116–17, 124, 126, 128–29, 133, 135

Franco-Soviet Pact: 104
Frederick the Great: 1, 137
Fröhlich, Paul: 72

Gaus: 131
Genoa Conference: 53, 55, 63–64
German-Soviet Trade Agreement:
  51
Goebbels: 117
Goltz, General von der: 13–16,
  22, 28, 92
Göring: 109
Great Britain (Britain, British):
  30–39, 55, 60, 73, 75, 77, 80,
  83, 85, 88, 93, 96, 98–99, 111,
  114, 117, 124, 126–28, 132–33,
  135

Haase, Hugo: 6–7
Halifax, Viscount: 122
Harden, Maximilien: 17
Hasse, General von: 58–60, 64
Haushofer: 58
Heilmann: 21
Helfferich: 2
Herriot: 77
Heydrich: 121
Hilferding, Rudolf: 7, 17, 25
Hilger, Gustav: 48
Hindenburg: 10, 11 n., 92, 108,
  122
Hintze, Admiral von: 21
Hitler, Adolf: 1, 9, 30, 68, 76, 91,
  98, 100, 104–109, 111–12, 114–
  15, 117–18, 120, 122–27, 129–
  31, 134–37
Hoffmann, General: 37, 68
House, Colonel: 8
Hugenberg: 105, 108, 112
Hughes, Charles E., 81
Hungary: 44

Ignatov: 3
Independent Social-Democratic
  Party, German: 6–8, 17–18, 42
Italy: 114, 126
Izvestiya: 51, 94, 109, 114

Japan: 80, 118–19, 126, 133, 136

Joffe, Adolf: 2–4, 63
Junkers: 56, 61

Kamenev: 118
Kapp (putsch): 28–31
Kautsky, Karl: 7
Kopp, Viktor: 48, 50–51, 57
Kornilov: 31
Krasin, Leonid: 49, 51, 57–58,
  60, 62, 76
Krestinsky: 51, 56, 60, 67, 119–
  20
Kronstadt rising: 38, 44
Krupp: 55–57, 59, 61, 68, 79
Kühlmann: 112
Kuomintang: 98

Labour Party, British: 98
Latvia: 14
Lausanne Agreement (1932), 104
League of Nations: 6, 62, 82–83,
  85–88, 97–98, 115, 117, 124–25
Lebedev: 59
Left Social-Revolutionary Party:
  2
Legien, Karl: 11, 29
Lenin: 7, 19, 25, 27, 29, 32, 39–
  40, 43–44, 47, 49, 54–55, 57–58,
  69–70, 76
Levi, Paul: 20, 42–45
Liebknecht, Karl: 7, 17
Lithuania: 14
Litvinov, Maxim: 63, 84, 86, 97–
  98, 100–101, 103–104, 109–10,
  114–15, 125, 129
Locarno Treaty: 67, 78, 82, 84–
  89, 91, 95, 117
Loucheur: 53
Ludendorff: 19–20, 22, 28, 68, 76,
  92
Ludwig, Emil: 102
Luther, Hans: 85
Lüttwitz, General von: 28, 92
Luxemburg, Rosa: 7, 17, 42

MacDonald, Ramsay: 77
Maltzan, Ago von: 62–64
March action: 42, 45–47

Manchester Guardian: 93
Manuilsky: 116
Marx, Heinrich: 86
Marx, Karl (Marxism, Marxist):
  3, 6, 20, 25, 31–32, 110
Menzhinsky: 57
Merekalov, 128–29
Ministry of War, German: 17–19,
  23, 57
Ministry of Marine, German: 61
Mirbach: 2
Moeller van den Bruck: 71
Molotov: 102, 110, 129–135
Mussolini: 124

Nadolny: 115
Narkomindel: *see* People's Com-
  missariat of Foreign Affairs
National-Socialist (Nazi) Party,
  German: 9, 88, 104–106, 108,
  111, 118
New Economic Policy (NEP):
  39–41, 46
Niedermayer, Oskar von: 58–59

Papen, Franz von: 104
People's Commissariat of Foreign
  Affairs (Narkomindel): 26, 34,
  69, 97, 129
People's Party, German: 28, 54,
  105
Philips Price, M: 18
Pilsudski, Marshal: 33, 34, 36
Poincaré, Raymond: 71, 102
Poland: 14, 33–39, 42, 48–49, 57–
  60, 70, 84, 86, 102–104, 110,
  115, 125, 128–36
Politburo: 55–56, 58, 60
Pravda: 3, 82, 94, 124

Radek, Karl: 3, 4, 8, 17–24, 37,
  42, 44, 46, 48, 54, 60, 62–63,
  65, 69–72, 74–75, 94, 115, 118–
  19
Rakovsky: 3, 62–63
Rapallo Treaty: 17, 40, 47–49,
  63–72, 74–76, 81–83, 86, 91,
  100–101, 103, 111

Rathenau, Walther: 9, 19–20, 53,
  62–65
Rauschning: 111
Rechberg, Arnold: 68, 112
Red Army: 33, 35–39, 48, 70,
  119–21, 127
Reibnitz, General von: 19, 22
Reichswehr: 11, 15, 22, 28–30,
  45–46, 58–59, 74–75, 92–95,
  107–108, 111–12, 120, 122–23
Reventlow: 71
Ribbentrop: 122, 134–35
Rosenberg, Alfred: 111
Rosenblatt: 60
Rote Fahn: 35, 71–72
Rumania: 104, 125
Rykov: 119

Scheidemann, Philipp: 93–95
Schlageter: 71–72
Schleicher, Kurt von: 11, 31, 58,
  75, 92, 108
Schnurre: 132
Schubert, Colonel: 58
Schulenberg: 125, 130–33
Seeckt, Hans von: 11, 15, 22–23,
  28–29, 31, 36–37, 56, 58–59, 64,
  66, 68, 70, 75, 80, 85, 92–93,
  95, 104, 108, 122
Selchow: 59
Simons, Hans von: 50
Sklyansky: 36
Skoblin: 120
Social-Democratic Party, Ger-
  man: 5–7, 9–10, 15, 18, 21–22,
  28–30, 32, 67–68, 72–75, 93–94,
  99, 106–108, 116
Sokolnikov, Grigori: 118
Spanish Civil War: 117
Spartakusbund: 6–7, 9, 42
Stalin: 72, 74, 76, 82, 97–99, 102–
  103, 115–16, 121, 124, 126–27,
  129, 134, 136
Stinnes, Hugo: 11–12, 52, 55, 68
Stolzenberg: 61
Stomonyakov: 51
Strasser, Otto: 105

Stresemann, Gustav: 9, 28, 52, 54, 68, 73, 75–76, 79–81, 83–90, 92, 96, 102, 105, 122

Talaat: 18
Thomsen, General von: 59
The Times (London): 35, 62
Tirpitz, Admiral von: 81
Trotsky: 35–37, 44, 47, 55–58, 72, 74–75, 106, 112
Tschunke, Major: 15, 58
Tukhachevsky, Marshal: 35, 118, 120
Turkey: 11, 18, 36

United Front: 43, 47, 72, 98
United States (America, American): 4, 21, 78–81, 87–88, 117, 126–27
Upper Silesian Plebiscite: 58, 62

Versailles Treaty: 15, 23, 27, 34–37, 39–40, 49–50, 55, 67–68, 85, 88, 95–96, 102, 115

Voroshilov: 134
Vorwärts: 93

Weizsäcker, Ernst von: 128–29, 131–32
Wiedenfeld: 52, 62
Wiedfeld: 79
William I, Kaiser: 1
William II, Kaiser: 1–3, 67, 87, 112–13, 137
Wilson, Woodrow: 6, 8
Winnig, August: 15
Wirth, Hans: 59, 62, 64, 66, 70
Wise, E. F.: 64
Wohltat: 132
Wrangel: 38

Zetkin, Klara: 28, 44
Zinoviev, Grigori: 38, 41–46, 69–70, 72–76, 97, 118
Zukunft, Die: 18, 23